I0015029

Personal Information Security & Systems Architecture

PII Techniques for Businesses

By

Keith A Marlow PhD BSc Hons MBCS MACS

Personal Information Security & Systems Architecture

PII Techniques for Businesses

By

Keith A Marlow PhD BSc Hons MBCS MACS

First published in 2018 by Aykira Pty Ltd. http://www.aykira.com.au/

Copyright © 2018 Keith Marlow.

 All rights reserved. Except as permitted under the *Australian Copyright Act 1968* (for example, a fair dealing for the purpose of study, research, criticism or review) no part of this publication may be reproduced, stored in a retrieval system, or transmitted in any form or by any means, electronic, mechanical, photocopying, recording or otherwise, without either the prior written permission of the publisher or a licence permitting restricted copying.

Cover images from Pixabay.

Personal Information Security & Systems Architecture
Marlow, Keith
ISBN (eBook): 978-0-6483501-0-1
ISBN (Print): 978-0-6483501-1-8

Disclaimer

The material in this publication is intended to act as a guide to how you approach information security concerning privacy and PII, and as such, you should endeavour to obtain independent professional advice to validate the application of this material to your situation before its usage. To the maximum extent permitted by law, the author and publisher disclaim all responsibility and liability to any person, arising directly or indirectly from any person or entity acting or not acting based on the information in this publication.

This book is dedicated to my father who encouraged my interest in computers at an early age. It's also dedicated to my wife, sons, family, and friends who gave me support and encouragement to explore this important topic.

PREFACE

"Personal Information security is everybody's problem."

From the software engineer to product manager, CTO, and CEO and the Board, all have a role in implementing well personal information security. Securing such personal information on computers is where this book comes into its own.

Globally, personal data breaches are at record levels. In 2017 identity theft, and related fraud cost $16 billion, affecting 6.7 million people, up 8% from 2016 (Javelin Strategy & Research, 2018). Generic cyber-attacks in APAC alone has cost an estimated $1.7 trillion in 2017 (Yu, 2018). The amount stolen is staggering; it's a multi-billion dollar "underground business" affecting everyone.

Concerning is the amount of personal data collected and exchanged. Facebook so far has over 300 petabytes (or 300,000 terabytes) of personal data (Vagata & Wilfong, 2014). Some argue this ability of businesses to collect vast amounts of personal data makes it easier for government agencies to spy on their citizens (Anderson, 2014).

People are waking up to the nightmare of wholesale collection and are either taking charge of their data, removing themselves from services (Twitter hashtag #DeleteFacebook for instance), or demanding action. Business leaders too are saying this cannot continue and are calling for well-crafted regulations when manipulating personal data (Apple, IBM chiefs call for more data oversight after Facebook breach, 2018) (Hoffman, 2018).

Governments, given such breaches and rampant wholesale data collection, are quickly creating robust legislation. Such legislation is in response to public and interest group pressure (Stella, 2017), with a focus on PII (Personally Identifiable Information).

Businesses, when faced with having to meet such evolving regulatory requirements, find it hard working out what to do; this is where this book excels. It explains what to focus on, when and why. Detailed are security, architectural and technical best practices based on real-world experience, combined with a PII focus – giving confidence that sensitive information is handled correctly.

This book also explores an approach to the problem of PII management and security. Rather than trying to deal with the problem case by case it's much better to produce an approach that puts to bed the issue of PII security. This is the only straightforward way to deal with the matter. Otherwise, the tide of PII breaches and misuse will continue.

It's important to note that this book does not adhere to any one standard or method, it's better to understand the way than say implement this because it's standard. This leads to a deeper understanding and a more likely outcome that the right decisions get made. Further, standards are not a pinnacle to reach. Instead, they are a level to reach and then exceed as needed to manage risks.

Remember, if standards compliance was all that's needed to be secure then why, given all the years of investment in security, are organisations suffering such enormous breaches across all sectors, both public and private? There is no substitute for understanding an area in depth and acting appropriately on it.

Keith Marlow

What This Book Covers

Chapter 1 What's PII and why all the fuss?

This chapter explains why all the concern around PII when businesses process it.

Chapter 2 Information Analysis

This gives an overview of what information is and defines what PII is.

Chapter 3 Regulations & PII

This chapter investigates the global regulations businesses will have to meet that relate to PII.

Chapter 4 Business Investment Case

Covers how to put together an investment case for addressing PII compliance obligations and what the skills set needs are to approach this.

Chapter 5 PII Discovery

Explains working out where PII exists in business systems.

Chapter 6 PII Analysis

This chapter covers working out the value of PII and what exceptional cases need addressing.

Chapter 7 Core Information Security Princip

This introduces the subject of information security with no prior knowledge assumed.

Chapter 8 PII Anti-Patterns

This chapter describes situations where PII isn't processed correctly or with inappropriate security controls.

Chapter 9 PII Strategies

Explains techniques on how to appropriately deal with PII.

Chapter 10 *PII Anonymisation*

Details standard mechanisms used to anonymise PII.

Chapter 11 *Putting it all Together*

This brings together all the work so far to implement a PII management solution.

Chapter 12 *The PII Vault*

Describes how to implement a single system to store PII that's suitably secured.

Chapter 13 *Future Trends*

Covers future developments in PII.

What is Not Covered

This book does not go into a detailed examination or explanation of the regulations and laws that impact a business with respect to PII and other sensitive information. If you are looking for legal nuances in how to interpret specific PII legislation, this is not the book for you, consult a good lawyer. It presents methodologies and technical solutions that aim by proper implementation to fulfil what the regulations demand.

That said, the laws that relate to PII are continually evolving, so do check on key issues covered in this book to see if still current when applied.

Who This Book is For

This book is equally for technical managers as well as software engineers, system architects, and consultants in any size of business. Although we expect the mid-sized business will get the most benefit, as they will have the most technical complexity with less unified oversight (too many spinning plates). If you are in the 'thick' of having to deal with the intersection of privacy, system architecture and security, you will find this book a gold mine.

Where warranted, parts of the book are highly technical. There are lots of references and explanations of terms to aid comprehension.

A background in information security isn't critical; core security concepts get explained from first principals in Chapter 7.

Usage & Support

This book is a handbook, so each Chapter you can dip into as needed. Although it is advisable to read it front to back at some stage, as the content interconnects and 'builds' as you progress through the book.

If you do find this book of use, please provide references back to it in your work. Securing computer systems is a problem we all share and the more we do to encourage the sharing and rewarding of ideas the better. Remember, we are not competing on security.

Also, if you have any comments, suggestions or are looking for help, please feel free to the contact the author (details at the back of the book). Also, visit https://www.aykira.com.au/books/ for more background information and additional resources.

Chapter 1
What's PII and why all the fuss?

There are known knowns.
There are things we know that we know.
There are known unknowns. That is to say, there are
things that we now know we don't know.
But there are also unknown unknowns. There are things
we do not know we don't know

Donald Rumsfeld, February 2002.

PII (Personally Identifiable Information) is defined as:

- Information that relates to a specific individual
- Information which is of a personally sensitive nature
- Information which should **not** get into the public domain

This definition is more encompassing than the more general definition (usually just the 1ˢᵗ clause above), as we want to focus on securing sensitive personal information; i.e. the information with value.

PII is often on computers, but it can be on other media (typically paper). What the information *is* and not *where* its stored is important.

Below are examples of what's considered PII:

- Full Name, address, email, and telephone numbers
- Date and place of birth
- Tax details
- Financial & Transactional Records
- Credit Histories and Scoring
- Legal and Government Records
- Identity documents: Passports, drivers licence, etc.
- Health & Mental Records

- Images or videos of a known person or persons
- Geolocation data (where someone has been)
- Biometric data (facial recognition, iris scans, fingerprints, voice prints, DNA, X-Rays, etc.)
- Vehicle Registration
- Web browsing history
- IP or MAC address
- Call histories
- Relationship details
- Private Correspondence

Given such variety, businesses have PII in their systems of which they were not aware. PII cuts across many different usage cases, even something as innocent as taking people's photos for profit (at a theme park ride or a wedding) could be PII if stored or indexed with other personal information.

Businesses collect PII for a variety of reasons, from customer details and past orders through to second by second interactions on a website. Businesses also receive PII when performing marketing activities, such as running competitions, loyalty schemes or sign-up programs.

Some businesses even collect PII to sell on, known as Data Brokerage and this helps businesses (for a fee) build lists of potential customers to target.

PII is just a Business Process Problem

Senior management considers PII from a top-down perspective as something dealt with via processes and a unified business approach to PII. On the face of it, that's correct; but it glosses over the technology, real world, and security aspects critical to how well the final processes work. Implemented wrong and the business has processes whose veracity is difficult to prove (if presenting specific logs and records in a court of law, how can they ensure the logs were unaltered?).

Processes also must be "human proof", otherwise they will not get actioned in the way expected, leading again to traceability problems and inefficiencies.

The devil is indeed in the detail on this.

Isn't This Just an ISMS?

An Information Security Management System (ISMS) can be an outcome of the PII analysis. So PII is in the ISMS, but PII is more than its security aspects, there may be PII with specific regulations beyond what an ISMS codifies.

> An ISMS defines policies and procedures for managing sensitive data to minimise risk and ensure business continuity by limiting a security breach impact using controls on employee behaviour, processes, data, and technology. See ISO 27001 for a specification.

Consider ISMS as a known tool in approaching PII security, but it should not be the only tool. For instance, an ISMS wouldn't consider the validity or appropriateness of how PII is used, yet in most regulations, this must be considered as a business cannot grab all the PII it wants.

Is This a PIMS?

A Personal Information Management System (PIMS) certainly covers what's done here, in that the result is a more systemized way of managing PII, with the ability for the individual to control whom accesses their information.

> Personal Information Management Systems (or PIMS) are systems that help give individuals more control over their personal data. PIMS allow individuals to manage their personal data in secure, local or online storage systems and share them when and with whom they choose. Providers of online services and advertisers will need to interact with the PIMS if they plan to process individuals' data. This can enable a human-centric approach to personal information and new business models.[1]

However, don't over-focus on developing a PIMS, the goal is to find a secure solution that works for just the business. Whether a PIMS is suited will depend on the amount of PII, the regulatory environments and the nature of the relationship with the customers; all investigated in more detail later.

Identity Theft & PII Misuse

If personal information about an individual gets into the wrong hands, it could result in:

- Takeover of the individual's identity;
- Then acting as the individual:
    - Use their credit cards or get new ones and then use them,
    - Take over their banking services and clear them out,
    - Take out a loan and run off with the money,
    - Sell their property out from under them!
    - Sell their shares, etc
    - Gain more PII for other people, and it carries on…

Such illegally obtained money often goes straight into the hands of criminals – it could even fund terrorist actions.

Such "identity theft" is universal and can range from simple online account takeovers to maxing credit cards to a complete hijack of a person's identity for use in fraud and money laundering.

Although to do a full hijack needs lots of information, it doesn't need gathering all at once, a cybercriminal can progressively build a profile over time working up into more sensitive sources of data until they hit the jackpot. Then with a complete profile, a cybercriminal can either use it for direct gain or sell it on the Dark Web for a profit. A whole online underground black market exists in PII and identities that trades 24 / 7.

---

[1]   https://edps.europa.eu/data-protection/our-work/subjects/personal-information-management-system_en

> A **cybercriminal** is someone who attacks and breaches computer systems for illegal gain. This is fundamentally a criminal undertaking in the majority case. The term 'hacker' isn't used in this book, the mass media has hijacked it to make reporting more dramatic; it really refers to the action of implementing a novel & interesting solution to a problem and doesn't have any negative overtones.

This is the real core of the problem, a single business may have PII which isn't enough to perform identity theft, but it's used to progress towards full identity theft. Hence why the reoccurring data leaks are so concerning. Parts of peoples' identity are continually leaking, and it just takes time to assemble.

To further complicate things, combining non-personal information can lead to PII discovery. For instance, just knowing someone's first name and date of birth will not enable identity theft, as many people have the same. But if stored with an address or telephone number, provided are the means to contact someone and gain more information (via social engineering, explained later).

PII gets stolen for many reasons:

- Financial benefit - A person's full identity ('fullz' in cybercrook lingo) on the Dark Web sells for over $1000 US.
- Political - Cambridge Analytica claims to have up to 5000 data points on 220 million Americans, used for "psychographic targeting".
- Reputational Damage

The political case is concerning, as there is evidence of illegally harvested PII was used as part of the 2017 US elections. The *thisisyourdigitallife* test app (allegedly) harvested Facebook friends' information which got sold on. In all, Cambridge Analytica used 50 million individual profiles to characterise US voters individually.

There is also the Doxing trend to worry about, especially with the impact on the wrong people or innocent parties by the information release and its consequences.

Doxing is the "compiling and releasing a dossier of personal information on someone". Originally done as a revenge tactic by cybercriminals in the 1990s, now adopted by groups like Anonymous as a key tactic.

Therefore, it's not just what information is held that decides if its PII, it's how much there is and what's done with it. The next chapter discusses this in detail as understanding the value of a piece of information is key to securing it.

How This Problem Came About

The finger on why there is such a PII problem gets pointed in many directions, but there are a few core drivers behind this:

1. Making computer systems secure gets perceived as hard, takes time and is expensive.
2. Computer systems evolve in response to requirements; businesses rarely have a blank slate to work with – so compromises and security gaps will develop, it's guaranteed.
3. New ways of attacking systems continuously evolve, what was secure degrades over time.
4. Keeping PII is desirable, given its perceived high business value.
5. Transferring data between computer systems in volume is easy, it's possible, in a few minutes, to transfer millions of records from one side of the globe to another. Therefore PII gets shared at a scale and rapidity never seen before.
6. Security is rarely baked-in to products and systems from the start, and the degree of support varies greatly and is often off by default (or there are easy to compromise defaults).
7. Computer systems are not designed from the ground up to differentiate in their treatment of PII and non-PII, there is no systematic 'awareness' of what's processed.

So over time, more interconnected systems process more PII, which results in a growing *security surface* to maintain. This, in turn, leads to an increased likelihood of breaches at progressively larger scales – sounds familiar?

> A security surface is an abstract surface or boundary at which security controls are employed, a bit like a castle wall it's the point where you start defending. A shorter wall is easier to defend than one which snakes all over the place and has the odd gap in it.

Software as a Service

Businesses offering cloud-hosted software services (SaaS providers) to other businesses are in a dangerous place, for several reasons:

- They have limited visibility into what PII is on their systems, and it changes all the time;
- They do not precisely know what regulations apply to them or their customers over time;
- If the service is hacked and PII leaks, the SaaS provider gets a big hit on bad PR. Yes, their customers suffered the loss, but the SaaS provider was instrumental in that loss and for the media, it's far more sensational (and easier) to say 10,000 customer accounts hacked from XYZ Inc in one front page article than 10,000 individual business articles.
- The individual businesses who suffered the loss will sue the SaaS provider for damages.
- Regulators will fine for breaches.

Add in that PII could be spread across multiple SaaS providers operating together, and it's a recipe for disaster (as strong as the weakest link). Interoperation on complex products between SaaS providers is the norm, as the product consists of distinct services or functions spread across instances on different SaaS provider networks. There is also great incentive of a SaaS provider to cross link or integrate with other SaaS products to increase their value offering. For example, a business uses an online accountancy product, that product, in turn, makes use of:

- **An Authorisation Service** – could be via OAuth[2] via Facebook or Google or some other cloud OAuth provider – they hold the core account details and the means to prove identity.

---

[2] OAuth (Open Authorization) is an open standard for token-based authentication and authorization online. This allows a single identity to reused securely across multiple products and services.

- **A payment gateway** – say Stripe or PayPal – this holds the payment and contact details.
- **An email gateway or mailing list service** – say MailChimp – this holds customer email addresses, names, and mailing preferences.
- **A user analytics service** – say Google Analytics – tracks how the product is used.

Each of these could be handling PII on behalf of the business customer via the accountancy product, and each of them needs securing for the entirety of the service to then be secure.

One could argue combining SaaS hosted services to implement a SaaS product is more secure, as there are more eyes, but it's a 50/50 thing. The fact that services are federated together means the security surface is something difficult to comprehend for any party. In effect, every business that uses any of the services can be in scope at the limit; it's a complex web of cloud interdependency. Therefore such a complex federated product is difficult to defend in complete confidence; it just takes one gap in the wrong place to result in a security breach, which is likely to impact multiple products at once.

Infrastructure as a Service

To add further confusion as to who owns or runs what, a business can rent space from Infrastructure as a Service (IaaS) providers directly, such as the likes of Amazon, Microsoft or Google. A business rents the provider's infrastructure (be that networks, servers, discs, etc.) and on top runs whatever service it needs, be that something built in-house or pre-packaged from another provider. It could even be that what the business buys and runs on the infrastructure, in turn, makes use of shared SaaS-based services (for example, remote backup services). This adds another dimension of complexity to the web of cloud interdependency.

So, online cloud services concerning PII are like Russian Dolls, a business needs to dig down into all the relationships to get a full understanding of where PII sits, who is responsible and where the risks lie.

The Internet of Things

One technology sector, which is causing concern in security circles (for a whole variety of reasons) is the Internet of Things (IoT) – these are internet connected devices which are cheap to manufacture, always on, always interacting with their environment and pushing information into the cloud real-time.

Such devices are capable standalone computers, so having them on any network is risky. Also, they are often associated with individuals, so can carry quite a bit of PII & privacy sensitive data on them. For instance, Fitness tracking app Strava recently (Feb 2018) caused a combined privacy & state level security problem when they mapped all their jogging activity on a heat map that revealed the locations of secret military bases as soldiers jogged around the bases.

Bolt on Security

A factor making it hard to keep information secure is that security has turned into a service business can call in as needed. This seems like a good thing, but it has resulted in security becoming a business and a large business indeed. Part of this ethos is that security is treated as an expert knowledge domain (a bit like going to the doctors), with its own technical language, techniques and tools.

So rather than treating the core problem (lack of knowledge, awareness, and responsibility), businesses buy in security solutions looking for a quick fix, which often they are not. Or instead, it fixes what's clear now, without adding the capability to the business to fix their own security issues.

There is another problem at play here, securing systems can become a prescriptive automated process: tools & techniques find security weaknesses to fix, and the process periodically repeats. Which can be a rather 'hands-off' way of implementing security, in that someone who's a security expert, yet not a technology expert, cannot 'pop the hood' of the system in question and find core security faults not otherwise evident. In other words, an insecure system could get a clean bill of health with internal weaknesses not discovered using tools from the outside. The expert will be unable (and unaware) to prove if the fixes truly address the core weakness (or doesn't introduce another). One could consider this a fault of process, oversight or resourcing; as systems need securing to the core.

There is also a danger here of 'tick-box security', in that a security agency runs through lists of checks to confirm compliance, often for a fixed fee; with clients who have little understanding what they are buying apart from a certificate of compliance. The client's focus is on getting that certificate of compliance; a failure to do so can mean a loss of business. So, the agency has little incentive to go actively looking for security faults beyond the strict interpretation of what's on the tick list, they want the repeat business and to get onto the next job.

Also, businesses starting out can consider security as something addressed when they reach a certain size. In other words, do the minimal security when starting, then plan to address the security deficit later when they have the time, money and resources to deal with it correctly. There are many cases where this does not pan out as intended, given the breaches start-ups suffer.

At the other end of the scale, at a large established business, it can be extremely hard to maintain a unified security approach using bought in security solutions. In effect, they buy in and apply security solutions on top of security solutions, which can be detrimental to effectiveness. For instance, a recent study found that 52% of Asia-Pacific companies with more than 50 different security products experienced higher incidents (Yu, 2018). Security by quantity alone is no substitute for quality.

The whole situation needs to change focus. Otherwise, information security will never directly address core problems, and the breaches will continue. Security, at its heart, is everybody's problem and therefore those who develop, support and design computer systems should all have extensive security training to 'bake in' security from the start. Just learning to code has *never* been enough. Security starts at the inside of systems, and that needs both strong technical and security skills to get right. Bolting on security to fundamentally insecure systems does **not** make them secure, it just 'preserves' the flaw for the cybercriminal to later discover.

Putting in security from the start may be a difficult challenge, as businesses usually gravitate to cheaper service providers. Hopefully, with the new wave of PII regulations, their eyes should open to the expensive risks they are taking by just focusing on costs.

Also, concerning the availability of knowledge, security experts are in high demand because there isn't enough of them, and there is just no substitute for experience in security and technology. Solving this supply problem needs a proper focus on education and mentoring and is in part the driver in authoring this book.

The Solution

Securing PII is a big problem, for several reasons:

- Hijacked stolen identities commit major crimes and move money around;
- It creates a massive remediation cost for governments, businesses, and individuals;
- It undermines trust in the services.
- There are lots of systems to fix.

Therefore, governments across the world are responding by putting in place legislation to ensure the handling of PII in a responsible manner by all actors. Ignorance of obligations will no longer be defendable; businesses must act appropriately and prove it.

Hence why the Donald Rumsfeld quote at the start of this chapter - there must be no unknown unknown's with how businesses deal with PII and secure it - complete awareness is a requirement going forward.

It is essential to understand the ramifications of this fully, in that before regulation compliance comes an ongoing 24/7 awareness of the PII in business systems and being confident that the processing of PII is always up to scratch. Otherwise, how is compliance & security assured?

What Happens if a Business does Nothing

It's not suggested to take this course of action, although let's play devil's advocate for a minute and see what could occur:

1. A business launches a new product online that has detailed registration information, as they need to know all they can about their customers to give them the best service possible.
2. Everything goes fine for the first six months, many tens of thousands of people registered from across the globe and the product is showing signs of really taking off.
3. The business gets a tip-off from a White Hat[3] that they have found a dump of the whole registration database on a Dark Web website for sale for just $750. It includes password hashes, names, addresses, etc. – everything.
4. *Panic Ensues*
5. The business gets the security hole fixed, just one line of code wrong.
6. After complaining about a lack of security culture in the business, the lead engineer quits!
7. The business CTO consults with the legal team and finds out because they have been taking registrations from multinationals, including Europeans and some other PII progressive countries, that they come entirely under their PII regulations (given the cloud deployment footprint).
8. Legal gives the advice that full disclosure is the only way to go otherwise the CTO would be negligent in their duties as a director and acting contrary to the PII regulations. No hiding this away.
9. The media get hold of the disclosure and to say the business suffers a PR media storm of biblical proportions would be an understatement.
10. The business gets fined and goes out of business, either due to the fines or because no one wants to be their customer anymore. The CTO might get struck-off as a company director or serve jail time

---

[3] A White Hat is a security consultant who is in on the good side, in that if they find a security flaw in a system they will notify the system operator first and not exploit it themselves. Conversely a Black Hat is the exact opposite.

depending on the data involved and how remiss the business was in handling the PII data.

This story may seem far-fetched and big-brother, but variations on this theme have occurred many times and are documented publicly[4]. The differences being the size & type of the organisation involved and if it weathers the storm (if the people involved can weather it is another matter, these sorts of events can end careers).

To show this isn't fiction, here are a few choice real-world examples:

- 198 million voter records exposed via public Amazon S3 server not correctly secured by Deep Root Analytics (June 2017)
- 143 million financial and credit reports hacked from Equifax (2017)
- 76 million financial records hacked from JP Morgan Chase (2014)
- 500 million user details from Yahoo (2014)

That is just a sample from a table of over 100 data breaches since 2004. The average cost of such breaches is in the order of $150 million by 2020 (Juniper Research, 2015). Hence why governments are acting on ensuring PII is appropriately treated by businesses, it has become a problem too significant to leave alone anymore.

So, in the end, doing nothing about PII will put a business at a severe operational & financial risk going forwards.

PII for Ransom

An unfortunate side effect to the strict regulations, with considerable fines, coming into force is that cybercriminals 'hold to ransom' the PII they discover (Ross, 2018). Knowing if they reveal the PII to the authorities the impacted business could face enormous fines and loss of market status. This is likely to first occur in Europe given the large fines businesses face there. We consider this a question of 'when' not 'if'. There is also no guarantee paying the cybercriminals off will prevent the breach being publicised.

---

[4] https://en.wikipedia.org/wiki/List_of_data_breaches

This is yet another darn good reason to do something about PII security as a priority.

PII Hype and FUD, The End is Nigh!

Something to be aware of is the hype and FUD[5] (Fear, Uncertainty, and Doubt) used by agencies and businesses to market their wares as one-stop solutions for dealing with PII in businesses.

Now if a business is small and has one or two systems to worry about, this could be a workable solution. Although if a business has any degree of complexity (and internal capability), such solutions could be somewhat "band-aid". In other words, they end up addressing the symptoms as they are now rather than the underlying issues. So, in the end, the PII management problem will later emerge demanding a proper solution.

They could also be solving a problem the business does not have or a problem more cheaply addressed by some other means. If the business does not do some level of PII analysis themselves (don't let the agency do it), they will not know if what was bought addresses key PII problems or not. Forewarned is indeed forearmed.

Efficiency Dividends

It's also worth considering that resolving PII technical issues in systems often results in better-understood dependencies and data flows, which can lead to operational efficiency improvements. You could find inefficient or quasi-bureaucratic processes at play or aged systems, which should be put out of your misery.

Removing data inefficiencies could have a dramatic impact on the business bottom line, for instance, it is reckoned a median Fortune 1000 company

---

[5] FUD was used originally by Gene Amdahl in 1975 to characterise IBM sales people tactics when he set up Amdahl Corp.

could increase its revenue by more than $2 billion a year if it increased data usability by just 10 percent (Maycotte, 2014). It's not all unwelcome news.

PII Security & Compliance, how do they fit?

Compliance is the act of a business complying with regulations or expectations of operation that come from the activities undertaken by a business. Successful compliance often results in certification to a given public standard, usually by an independent certifying third party.

Shown below is how this all relates to PII Security.

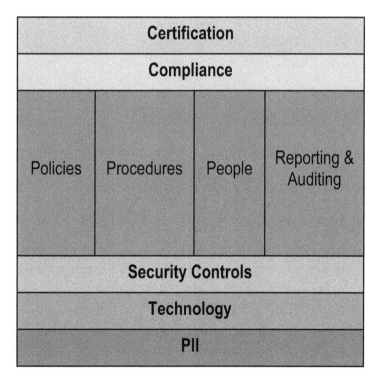

Figure 1 - The PII and Compliance Stack

As shown above, PII 'sits' at the bottom behind what technology its held in and accessed by. Next up are the Security Controls that ensure only those permitted to interact with the PII can do so. Above that are the actual business Policies that map down into Procedures often implemented by People and the Reporting and Auditing mechanisms used to ensure correct implementation of the policies. Above these is the actual mechanism that manages compliance (Compliance Officers and senior management) and the final (potentially public) certification of compliance.

So, in a way compliance sets the stage for what PII Security should achieve to support the compliance requirements. The compliance operation does not define 'how' to enact the Security Controls around PII just what the expected outcome should be in terms of risk management. Compliance is just another requirement on systems to account for.

Also, compliance is not the only driver for PII Security, it may be the initiator, but the security of PII needs specific consideration beyond what pure compliance demands, as you will see later.

PII & Privacy, are they related?

Privacy & PII are very much related. Privacy is where people want to keep their actions & information private from third parties (such as businesses and governments) and in some cases be effectively anonymous and unknown. What people think is private differs significantly between cultures and individuals, but it all stems from the universal desire for privacy.

PII is information that an individual either wants to keep private or control who has access to it in a very deliberate way. The mechanisms to enact privacy have a lot of commonalities to those used to keep PII private and protected.

Looking after PII is an act of keeping it private from those who should not access it; although privacy isn't the same thing, it's closely related to PII regarding how an individual would want to treat it. Such a mindset is useful to have, privacy and PII are in effect opposite sides of the same *personal* coin, one looks to hide and be anonymous, the other protects.

Privacy & Security, are they related?

Privacy and security are very much related. It will be exceedingly difficult to achieve privacy without applying the appropriate security controls. Security comes into play in not only the physical realm (locks, cameras & access controls) it also features heavily in the digital realm as well (encryption, anonymisation, access controls and monitoring).

Any consideration of privacy enactment must be professionally covered by specific consideration of the appropriate security controls that must be applied. In other words, trying to construct a privacy framework without immediate consideration of what security techniques apply is a risky undertaking. Hence why in this book effort is taken assessing and valuing PII and then protecting it using proven security techniques; how can you expect to keep something private if you do not know it's worth to others?

Key Points

- Businesses have more PII than they think.
- Cybercriminals can combine PII over time to perform identity theft.
- Most identity theft revolves around financial fraud.
- Data breaches involving PII are common.
- Cybercriminals see regulatory fines as an opportunity to hold businesses to ransom.
- Watch out for the hype!
- Tidying up PII processes can bring significant operational rewards.
- Compliance in businesses often drives PII Security but does not define it.

Personal Information Security & Systems Architecture

- Governments are mandating the proper treatment of PII and businesses have little choice but to comply.

Chapter 2
Information Analysis

You can have data without information, but you cannot have information without data.

Daniel Keys Moran

We live in an information-rich world; information overload is a real problem. So which information is worth caring about? For an individual and a business, information, and the data from which it comes has different qualities and value. Not all information is equal, but data is worthless until it becomes information.

This chapter looks at what it takes to turn data into information, its inherent value and its distinct types, then whether it is something worth caring about and hence securing, and when the information finally becomes PII.

When Data Becomes Information

Is there data or information to work with? Too often it's assumed that one is the other or that they are interchangeable, they are not. One definition is:

Data is how something is stored or transmitted, while information is something that can be understood by people and then in turn usefully processed by a computer.

Now that definition on its own doesn't help much from a value and security point of view; it appears the context in which data is *seen* determines if it's information – which isn't correct.

This book uses the following definition:

Information is facts which have a value to being processed and utilised. Data is how you choose to store or exchange such information.

This definition recognises that information can have different values depending on its use and who is using it. For instance, the number 123456 on its own is just a number, with no real value, while if that were the code to open an insecure gold bullion safe, that would suddenly have significant value. So, the relationship or connection with another piece of information (the safe), on the underlying information (the number) can grant it dramatically more value than it had before.

Regarding PII this is an important concept to understand, as what a business considers its value could be radically different to what its public value is (discussed later).

Information has value

As mentioned, information has value, determined by the following qualities:

- **Application**
- **Correctness**
- **Timeliness**
- **Uniqueness**
- **Relevance**

Previously discussed was the **application** quality, the information could equally be the keys to the kingdom or the keys to the broom cupboard, which cannot be determined without the context of application. Now, this might be self-evident, as "12-34-56 9876543" looks a lot like a bank account number, but usually without context all that is known is the type of information it is, not to what it relates.

Correctness is a concept that information needs to be correct to be useful, if that code were "987654" and hence wrong, we would only find out it had no value[1] until trying to use the code. Which implies the way information is stored or transmitted, needs to preserve its correctness always. Information that rots in storage or gets garbled when communicated is no good to anyone.

Timeliness refers to if the information has a time window of usefulness and hence value. Usually, the older information is, the less useful it is, it's superseded by something more up-to-date. A classic example is the price of a share, its price right now has an incredibly high information value (especially when now is sub-second availability) but the price a few hours ago is virtually worthless.

Uniqueness also works equivalently, a single copy of a critical piece of information that nobody else has (and this is known to be the case) could have an incredibly high information value. For example, if a business could get the most up to date share price from a stock market, they have an incredible trading advantage over their competition as they will be able to get in ahead of them.

Which is where such unique information becomes an instant competitive advantage; the business knows something their competition does not at a useful time. Also, uniqueness can be a quality of information that needs preserving, for instance, privileged defence documents in a court case must remain private and restricted in their circulation for the legal process to work as intended.

Finally, for information to have value, it must have **relevance** to something that in of itself has recognised value. There is no point knowing all there is about the breeding habits of web-footed gecko's if not used to advantage. Although this needs careful consideration, as relevance ties closely to the application; it might have no value to a business if they cannot see a way to derive value, yet to some other business with a new application it could be valuable (anyone for a TV series on gecko's?). Such a situation is where businesses often undervalue what's PII, as with more information it can suddenly become valuable, and boy do the bad guys know this.

---

[1] One could also argue that incorrect information has negative value, in that it corrupts all that it touches.

Information Value Informs Design

Knowing the value or potential value of information allows the determination of:

- The best way to store or handle such information as to preserve or maximise its value;
- The proper way to secure such information to stop others from obtaining it and then obtaining its value or using it to obtain more value.

Knowing the value of information can guide the system architecture, storage technologies, processes, procedures, and security measures employed to ensure only the owning business derived value from it and nobody else.

Which may seem a strange way of looking at things, but it's key to gaining an awareness of what information is flowing through systems and hence why the need to pay attention to reducing security and hence business risks. It could be, for example, that a business has members of staff dealing with high-value information who are unvetted or not trained to be dealing with it correctly and securely; without such information value analysis discovering this as a problem will be extremely hard.

PII Value Perspectives

Information value has three perspectives, as shown below:

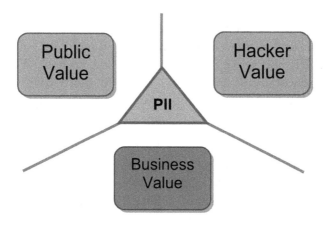

Figure 2 - PII Value Perspectives

The business value is the value placed by a business on its PII for its use. The public value is what the public consider the value of their PII and the cybercriminal value is the value the cybercriminal could derive from that PII if given a chance to do so.

So what order would you have those, with the highest value at the top and the lowest at the bottom? You could do:

1. Business Value
2. Cybercriminal Value
3. Public Value

Seems reasonable, but it's wrong. Most businesses overvalue their PII (for reasons given later) and undervalue its value to cybercriminals and the public.

Personal Information Security & Systems Architecture

A somewhat more realistic order is as follows:

1. Cybercriminal Value
2. Public Value
3. Business Value

Remember the value is what's extracted from the PII, not what business considers it might be worth. A cybercriminal has no difficulty selling on PII to all and sundry; they can quickly extract the highest value from every single bit of PII and move onto the next system to hack. The public as a rule value privacy and hence PII, certainly more than perceived by businesses. Also, the public value is influenced strongly by the media cycle and public feelings, so can wax and wane quickly.

About the low value of PII to a business; typically, a business must combine the PII with some service or product to create value; the PII on its own to a business isn't valuable without doing something with it. Businesses also incur the costs of having to support, secure and keep the PII up to date, which are considerable. Additionally, the business can usually only do one thing with it, while the cybercriminal or public value of PII is seen through the lens of its total extractable or potential value.

What's also interesting is that each of the three perspectives often has truly little real understanding of the value of PII compared to the other two - one could say this is a large part of the problem.

Risk Assessment Skew

For a business this difference in the apparent value of an information asset can be quite dangerous. Most mature businesses as part of a structured approach to risk management perform a Risk Analysis, in which all assets are valued, all the threats to those assets are established and their respective probabilities. This feeds into an understanding of the amount of tolerable loss per year and hence what safeguards, countermeasures and actions need undertaking.

Yet, as shown above, the probability of occurrence of a threat will be out, as the business is considering that probability based on what it considers the value of information, not its value to the cybercriminal. This will result in an underinvestment in compensating security controls around PII, even at the most formalised businesses.

There is also the risk that such wrong valuing of an information asset could go undetected as its part of a larger information asset itself. For instance, a user record could contain high value PII fields, and only considered is the whole record value in the analysis, not the component fields.

Some Risk Analysis methodologies try to account for this indirectly by considering the costs of embarrassment or legal/regulatory costs, but again this is prone to the businesses view of what their exposure to embarrassment or imposed fines is; if they do not have fine detail from which to derive a quantitate value of an information asset, they are at risk of missing it.

Relationship of PII to Trust

For a business to manipulate PII, its trusted by the individuals for whom it has PII. Trust isn't an absolute measure; there is no fixed point at which a business becomes trusted, it depends on many factors beyond just the use of PII. Keep in mind that PII exists in a hierarchy of trust as shown below.

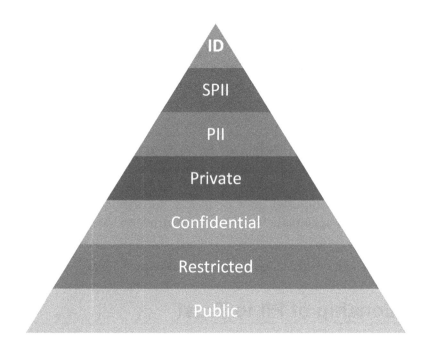

Figure 3 - Information Trust Pyramid

At the very top of the Information Trust Pyramid is a person's actual ID or identity, what makes them an individual and how they prove their identity. When dealing with a person's direct identity and how they prove it to others, a business or organisation needs to be extremely trustworthy in a constantly provable way (hence why governments undertake this).

Next down is what's termed SPII, this is a subset of PII and refers to PII that is especially sensitive (such as medical or criminal records, more later), which again needs an exceedingly high level of trust to work with. Next down is regular PII, this also needs a high degree of trust. Next is information which is Private and then Confidential, the difference being Private information is just known to a person (say a journal) and Confidential is by design and often has legal ramifications around it (say a contractual document). Which implies that what's Confidential isn't necessarily PII; they can differ. Restricted information gets shared with a known group of people, and Public is available to all.

This hierarchy does not mean that what's in the public domain is untrusted; it just comes with no controls that proves or requires trust to access.

The critical take away from this diagram is the higher a business works on the pyramid; they can expect more regulations and more risks to mitigate by the progressive application of stricter security controls. Such controls cannot be: simplified, sidestepped, or streamlined; they are risk appropriate by design. Also, businesses can expect the damage caused to reputation by a breach to be higher. In effect, these are the inescapable costs of having to maintain trustworthiness with personal data in your systems.

When Information Becomes PII

Now that a way of classifying information by where it comes from and how it's used is defined, next is deciding when information turns into PII and how to deal with it.

The key concept is that PII is enough information to identify an individual with certainty and discover something sensitive about that individual.

So, onto some worked examines, for each consider if just the information given on its own is PII. Let's go:

Fred Bloggs

That is **not** PII, a person's name on their own is public knowledge and does not to lead to a unique individual. Remember it's just the name on its own and nothing else.

Personal Information Security & Systems Architecture

Fred Wilberforce Bloggs, Kentucky

Now, this is PII, as it's just enough to uniquely identify the individual, given the use of a full name and the state.

15 Data Drive, Dartmoor

Tricky, who is at that address, could be a factory or a cottage? Although, purely on its own it's not PII.

15/5/1981

Just a date, so on its own it's **not** PII.

15/5/1981, Kentucky

Again, it's not PII, it's just a date and place, a lot of things happened on the 15/5/1981 in Kentucky.

DOB 15/5/1981

Okay, so that date is a Date of Birth, but it doesn't say whose date of birth it is – lots of people were born on that day and given there is nothing else – it's not PII.

DOB 15/5/1981, Kentucky

So, we have a date of birth and the state of Kentucky; again it's reasonable to assume lots of people were born on that day in Kentucky – so it's not PII.

Fred Bloggs, DOB 15/5/1981

Now that is PII, as it resolves to just one person.

Male, 21045, DOB 15/5/1981

So, we know someone's sex, ZIP code, and date of birth. That is technically PII, 87% of the population of the United States is found with just that alone[2]. You should be surprised by that, and this is something to learn to watch out for.

Now for a tricky one.

info@abusiness.com

It's an email address, so it looks like it's not PII, but if it was part of a record, like:

Fred Bloggs, info@abusiness.com

Then it becomes PII, but what about just the following:

Fred.bloggs@abusiness.com

To the computer, it's just an email address, but a human can parse out of that the person's name – the fact the name can be extracted makes it PII.

Emails are difficult as within the email address is it possible to encode personally identifiable information – so unless there is 100% confidence the email isn't related to any other personal data, it's treated as PII (although it's not highly valued PII). Also, remember that knowledge of an email address could allow the gathering of more PII via a web search or by contacting the individual.

With the email address, it's possible even to try to gain access to the email account itself (for most email hosting services use standardised means of access) and discover yet more PII and other exciting information (maybe PII about other people?). In most cases getting *into* someone's email account, for a savvy cybercriminal, is like hitting a PII jackpot. This all depends on what other information was with the email address.

---

[2] Comments of Latanya Sweeney, Ph.D. on "Standards of Privacy of Individually Identifiable Health Information"". Carnegie Mellon University.

Personal Information Security & Systems Architecture

Now what about:

-33.868820, 151.209296

That is a latitude and longitude, which on its own isn't PII. But what about:

-83.92496114,35.95504011
-83.92496114,35.95697057
-83.92224017,35.95697057
-83.92224017,35.95504011
-83.92496114,35.95504011

Again, it's not PII, nothing personal about it. Let us try:

Fred Bloggs, 12/2/18, 13,15,
-83.92496114,35.95504011
-83.92496114,35.95697057
-83.92224017,35.95697057
-83.92224017,35.95504011
-83.92496114,35.95504011

Now that can be PII, given it looks like it holds a name, a date and a time and a GPS path – so it could be a person's movements at that given time, which they could repeat again or indicate where they live or work.

Now what about:

4518 1234 1234 1234

That's a credit card number, so can uniquely track an individual or entity in many different contexts across different businesses – yet it doesn't indicate which individual, so it is not PII on its own

It should be very rare indeed to encounter such credit card information *in the plain* (encoded in plain text and readable from a storage medium without needing decryption). The PCI standards exist to safeguard and ring-fence such data and prevent its use outside the context of a pure payment mechanism (so credit cards used for indexing individuals indicates a significant security problem).

Now for a trickier one:

42d1a9b9-7340-4ce0-a79a-3447859314bc

That weird looking string of characters is a GUID, a Globally Unique Identifier; it's a 128-bit integer used to index some resource with a high guarantee that two generated GUID's for different resources won't clash (be the same) for a long enough time to not to have to worry about it.

Is that GUID PII or not purely on its own? It's not PII, as knowing just that without its context of use reveals no information about whether it refers to an individual or an order for flowers. In fact, knowing it refers to an individual gets an attacker nowhere if they cannot query the system holding the PII; and this is where GUID's are useful, in that they provide a way to refer to an individual without giving anything away about them (more about this later).

What about this?

Ms. Davis is a 45-year-old woman with past medical history that includes a pilonidal cyst. This was removed when she was 19. Last July she presented with more pain in this area. On exam, it was unclear if there was a recurrence. She was put on a course of Keflex and everything resolved. She presents to walk-in today saying that same thing has happened. She has had a couple of days of increased swelling in this area. No fevers. Mild pain. Bowel movements are fine.

Is it PII or not? On the face of it, the only personal identifiers in there are Ms. Davis and her age – which *could* identify an individual; and this is the crux if there are enough datums to identify an individual then it's PII. It's not left to chance that a person is identified, either they can be (it's PII) or not. This situation is where a lot of people get classifying PII wrong. Therefore it's essential to understand this crucial point.

Also, in this case, given the text is of a medical nature, there could well be other regulations that come into play.

Now what about:

Mr John Doe, 1A Dead Place, Nowhere, 9999

Is that PII? If you thought yes, you are wrong unless there is a Dead Place in Nowhere. It's deliberately incorrect information <u>not</u> associated with an individual by design. This situation occurs most often with test data which is machine generated.

Although if its machine-generated, there could be a small risk that by accident created is some information matching to an individual – given the data's used only in a test situation and therefore never makes it into production, this should not be an issue.

Linked Information and cross-indexing risks

There is another critical situation concerning PII. Often information on an individual is spread across many different systems and databases. Each of these does not hold enough information to be PII, yet via some common key or link, the systems can be accessed and then the results combined to get a view which is undoubtedly PII sensitive (M. Schwartz, 2011). Such building of identity from multiple sources is known as re-identification and is something to be genuinely concerned about.

For instance, given a database that holds postal addresses (in some mailing system) and then another system which holds names (a marketing database) – each is not PII. Yet, if brought together, for a mail merge, then the system performing the mail merge is dealing with PII information. It might be that the mailing list goes to a 3rd party to do the mailing run – the question then becomes are they PII compliant and what happens to that mailing list when done? Do they delete all trace of it, or do they store it and sell it on?

Also, such linking or aggregation need not occur via systems under the control of one business. For instance, there may be two systems, each with their own keying mechanism, and a third system that happens to be in the public domain (a website indexed by a search engine) which can map between these two keying mechanisms. This same situation can even occur when visiting two websites, one where entered is a name and address, the other where this isn't done, the second website can use the IP address of the browser to map back to the name and address entered in the first web site. Also, the increased usage of social media tracking technologies on websites (activity feeds, targeted ads, etc. which track using shared cookies) gives another mechanism to enable such a mapping.

In fact, search engines are quite powerful PII discovery mechanisms, individual bits of personally sensitive information can combine into a search query, and there is a chance the associated individual is found right away, or more information detection occurs that enables their discovery against other information sources.

There have also been cases of researchers making use of large publicly available data sets (such as a photo on a social website) categorising the data and then using it to do a reverse lookup to discover an individual[3]. There have even been examples of individual identification based on online public movie reviewing behaviour on IMDB compared to private movie reviewing behaviour on Netflix (Shmatikov, 2008).

This problem also does not need to exist now. Rather, the potential is there for the linking or aggregation to occur in the future. So, by implication, things need to either be set up now so that can never happen or admit defeat now and declare all these personal parts as PII.

Weak Anonymisation

Another unintended source of PII can come from when PII is weakly anonymised, in that enough information's left so that with careful analysis it's possible to rediscover the individual. It may not be immediately evident that such an analysis could be successfully performed.

---

[3] Egor Tsvetkov, a student at the Alexander Rodchenko School of Photography in Moscow photographed people sat opposite him when he rode the Metro. He then used an app to find the person's social media page on VK, a Russian social media site. (April 2016)

The classic example of this is the 2006 release by AOL of 20 million search queries for the benefit of researchers, which were meant to be fully anonymised. It didn't take a team of reporters long to discover the information could be used to find out exactly who did some of the searches. They were able to find that User 4417749 was a 62-year old widow who lived in Lilburn GA (Michael Barbaro & Tom Zeller, 2006).

The dangers of progressive system change

Another issue that crops up is with multiple systems that have evolved with respect to what information they are collecting and processing. It could be that over time the precise understanding of what's contained in each system is lost or obscured, leading to a situation in which you fall into dealing with PII without knowing it.

This situation is a lot more common than people realise because of the *limited horizon effect*. This effect is where an individual (or team) can only deal with keeping up to date with so much at a time and remain effective (they must do their day job as well). Also, how far out they can remain correct concerning their context depends on their workload and the rate of change experienced. So, in a business with continuous ongoing technical change, requires specific efforts to mitigate this effect. Or look at it the opposite way, a business that encounters a lot of change and does nothing to counter the limited horizon effect specifically – there will be unknown gaps in knowledge and therefore a high chance of inappropriate PII manipulation.

Key Points

- Information is facts that have value when processed and utilised.
- Data is how we choose to store or exchange such information.
- Information has a value to a business and can have a vastly different public value.
- Information value comes from its application, correctness, timeliness, uniqueness, and relevance.

- Knowing the value allows the determination of how to store or handle information and how to secure it.
- The degree of information trust required of a business handling sensitive information or identities is directly proportional to the security controls required.
- Many types of PII exist, some not immediately apparent.
- Some PII needs specific treatment.
- Crossed linking information or aggregating can create PII out of thin air.
- Publicly available data sets and search engines allow methods of discovery not previously possible.
- Weak anonymisation of PII can allow individual discovery.
- Be aware of the dangers of progressive system development and your horizon letting PII creep in.

Chapter 3
Regulations & PII

The thing we have to be careful of is that the Internet is a global communications medium, and if one country tips the balance in regulating its use or regulating what companies or individuals do on the web, it could have an economic impact that might be unintended, quite frankly, by the regulations themselves.

John W. Thompson

As previously mentioned, governments are tightening up how businesses and organisations handle PII to combat the wave of privacy breaches and the associated damages to people's identities. Another driver for this is that identity theft is utilised by organised crime to hide or put at arm's length illegal activities, virtual "identity mules" if you will.

The methods taken by governments range from non-existent, to the enlightened and through to the positively scary; creating an extreme headache for a business, because:

- The rules when PII regulations apply differ and depend on what businesses do, where they do it and whom they are working with.
- What businesses do and whom they do it with and where continually changes.
- Such regulations are NOT set in stone, some have been around for years, others keep getting tweaked, and some are so new they haven't even been tested in court yet.
- The extensive usage of cloud SaaS solutions adds another complication, how does one know they are compliant with PII regulations? Figuring out who is compliant can be quite hard as certain SaaS providers do not want to commit to a definitive PII position (no idea why they do this, as stating wilful ignorance is no defence). Also, even if they state compliance now, given

technology change and their use of 3rd parties, how can one be sure they will be compliant going forwards (remember the Russian Dolls)?

- Equivalently, usage of 3rd party software solutions, or allowing others to interface their systems into your business systems creates compliance visibility and enforcement problems.

As a result, it's not a question of if a business will encounter PII regulation, it's more a matter of which ones need abiding by.

In this chapter we look at the major PII regulations currently in operation to show their variety, we then explain the common 'roots' that can then later be used to create a common approach to compliance & security.

PII Regulations are not Alone…

Businesses need to comply with other information processing regulations to trade in certain sectors. Such regulations come under Information Governance where needed are methods of record keeping with Policies and Procedures. Listed below are some of the main sectors where this occurs:

- Medical and Health Services
- Financial Services
- Credit Card Processing
- Military & Police Services
- Government Services

Such regulations are in addition to any other regulations or policies, such as background checks, qualifications, permits, liquidity, insurance, standards compliance, etc. Also, if implementing ad hoc financial transactions between third parties, there might be a need to comply with fraud detection and money laundering reporting requirements in most mature economies.

So PII & privacy needs considering along with all these other regulations, although the good news is that the security requirements often fit together well with these regulations, just ensure there are no expensive gaps in coverage.

PII Regulations In Force

The following is a list of the principal government-sponsored PII Regulations in force internationally (this list isn't exhaustive as new regulations are coming into force all the time):

- Europe - **General Data Protection Regulation (GDPR)**
  - o Supersedes and automatically applies to all member states.
  - o Controls collection, storage, access, deletion and sharing of PII
  - o Stiff penalties enforced for none compliance.
  - o Comes into full force 25th May 2018
  - o Potentially global remit
- UK - **Data Protection Act**
  - o Implements the EU Directive on the protection of personal data
  - o Although given Brexit, this will need replacing at some point
- Australia - **Privacy Act**
  - o Similar intent to the GDPR although not as 'strict'.
  - o Mandatory data breach reporting came into effect on 22nd Feb 2018.
- Canada – **Personal Information Protection and Electronic Documents Act (PIPEDA)**
  - o Compliance with EU data protection law
- Switzerland – have their own laws which partially implement the EU Data Protection Directive to encourage free trade.
- USA – no single unified law as concerns PII. Rather, case by case legislation covers specific sectors and circumstances. The U.S. Federal Trade Commission (FTC) will often step into the breach if a business is wanting in handling consumers personal information in a secure way. There is also the U.S. Privacy Act of 1974, but

that's based in the old paper-based ways of manipulating information. There is also state-based legislation to consider (Data Breach Notification Laws across 47 states, California first is 2002).

Next, shown in depth, is the variety of legislation in force and hence how careful a business needs to be, lots of traps everywhere.

Note: In the regulations there is often reference to 'Personal Data', treat this as PII.

Terminology

To help with understanding the regulations, defined here as some of the terms used:

- **Data Subject** – the individual whose Personal Data is in a system.
- **Data Controller** – this is an entity which determines what processing occurs on the Personal Data and they usually have a direct relationship with the Data Subject.
- **Data Processor** – this is an entity that processes personal data on behalf of a Data Controller.
- **Supervisory Authority** – the government authority charged with enacting privacy legislation in a given jurisdiction.

Europe – General Data Protection Regulation

The goal with the GDPR is to unify data protection for individuals in the EU and control the export of personal data outside of the EU. Which, in turn, *should* simplify the regulations for businesses. It came into full force across Europe (and the World) on the 25th May 2018.

Its key points are:

- Must appoint a Data Controller and an (optional) independent Data Protection Officer to aid with compliance actions, depending on the volume and type of personal data processed.

- Provide notice for personal data retention period and contact details for Officers.
- The right to contest automated decision-making, including profiling[1].
- Demonstrate GDPR compliance by design and by default
- PII processing can only occur if there is a lawful basis for doing so and consent is given by the data subject to do so. Specific consent must be sort for optional services, rather than a blanket 'consent to all or no longer use' technique. Legal guardians need to give consent for children under 16.
- Privacy policies must be easy to read and detail all usage cases of personal data[2]. A change in usage requires notification and agreement.
- Data subjects have a right of access (data display service), a right of complete erasure[3] ('Right to be forgotten'), a right to stop processing their data[4] and a right to transfer their data to another service (data export service). This includes propagating the changes or deletion to 3rd parties as required.
- The GDPR defines Data Controllers and Data Processors. A Data Controller determines the purpose or methods of processing. A Data Processor provides infrastructure or services for Data Controllers to utilise. Both have legal obligations to protect personal data and are liable for data breaches. A business can be both at the same time. Data Controllers need to review their Data Processors for compliance.
- Businesses undertaking large-scale data processing, profiling or activities with a high risk to rights and freedoms of people need to conduct a Data Protection Impact Assessment (DPIA)[5].
- Keep logs of data processing activities and make available to the supervisory authority on request. Data Processors need to keep

---

[1]   https://advisera.com/eugdpracademy/gdpr/automated-individual-decision-making-including-profiling/
[2] https://advisera.com/eugdpracademy/gdpr/conditions-for-consent/
[3] https://gdpr-info.eu/art-17-gdpr/
[4] https://advisera.com/eugdpracademy/gdpr/right-to-restriction-of-processing/
[5] https://advisera.com/eugdpracademy/gdpr/data-protection-impact-assessment/

logs of whom they processed data for and how and if transferring data to a third country or international organisation.

- Data breaches of PII are notified to the Supervisory Authority without delay (within 72 hours). Data subjects only need notifying directly if the data breach was 'readable'. i.e. plain text and not encrypted.

- Sanctions range from a written warning, regular audits, up to 20m EUR or 4% of annual worldwide turnover, whichever is the higher[6].

When does the GDPR impact?

As a rough rule of thumb, a business may have to comply if:

- The business has an office in the EU, *OR*,
- The business has a website that allows EU customers to order goods or service in a European language (other than English) or enables payment in Euros[7], *OR*,
- The business website mentions customers or users in the EU[8], *OR*,
- The business tracks individuals in the EU via the Internet and uses data processing techniques to profile individuals to analyse and predict personal preferences, behaviours or attitudes[9].

If a business must comply, they will have to appoint a representative in an EU member state to act as a point of contact for supervisory authorities and individuals to ensure compliance with the GDPR.

Information the GDPR applies to

The GDPR applies to "personal data" which is "any information relating to an identified or identifiable natural person". This information includes, but not limited to: their name, home address, email address, bank details, posts on social networking websites, medical information or a computer's IP address.

---

[6] https://www.gdpreu.org/compliance/fines-and-penalties/
[7] Recital 23, GDPR
[8] Recital 23, GDRP
[9] Recital 24, GDRP

More protections also apply to "special categories" of personal data:

- Racial or ethnic origin;
- Political opinions;
- Religious or philosophical beliefs;
- Trade union membership;
- Genetic or biometric data for uniquely identifying a natural person, and,
- Data about a natural person's sex life or sexual orientation.

The handling of such data cannot occur unless one of the following exemptions[10] apply:

- Explicit Consent is given unless prohibited by other laws;
- Data controller or subject operates in the field of employment, social security or social protection;
- It is in the vital interests of the data subject (or another natural person) where the data subject cannot give consent (physically or legally incapable);
- Data subject is a member (past or current) of the data controlling organisation with a political, philosophical, religious or trade union aim;
- The data has been publicly disclosed;
- Part of legal proceedings;
- In the substantial public interest;
- For the purposes of preventive or occupational medicine;
- For the reasons of public interest in the area of public health;
- For the archiving purposes in the public interest, scientific or historical research purposes or statistical purposes.

Note: GDPR defines biometric data as "personal data resulting from specific technical processing relating to the physical, physiological or behavioural characteristics of a natural person, which allow or confirm the

---

[10] https://gdpr-info.eu/art-9-gdpr/

unique identification of that natural person, such as facial images or dactyloscopic (fingerprint) data".

Member State Differences

Member states may layer on more legislation to suit their legislative needs. For example:

- On the death of an individual in Spain, the heir's entitled to access, rectification or deletion of data held by information society service providers.
- In Ireland, there will be an exemption from many of the rights and obligations provided under the GDPR for data processed for journalistic purposes or academic, artistic or literary expression where compliance with such provisions would be 'incompatible' with such purposes.
- In Germany, there is a requirement for a general framework for the processing of sensitive data, including rules on health data (no explicit restriction to genetic/biometric data). Such processing is only possible if taking "suitable and specific" safeguards to protect data. The safeguards may include technical and organisational measures, pseudonymisation, encryption, or the appointment of a Data Protection Officer (DPO) etc.
- The UK is introducing two new penalties:
    - Re-identifying anonymised or pseudonymised data;
    - Altering records with intent to avoid responding to a subject access request.

UK – Data Protection Act

The UK Data Protection Act 1998 protects personal data stored on computers or in an organised paper filing system. It follows the EU Data Protection Directive and does not apply to domestic use. It implements a set of rights and principals. Once the GDPR comes into force, the DPA will be repealed and replaced by one act covering the GDPR and how it integrates into UK law.

Personal Rights

Under the act an individual can:

- View the data an organisation holds for a reasonable fee;
- Request the correction of incorrect information;
- Require that no data is used in any way that may potentially cause damage or distress;
- Require that their data isn't used for direct marketing.

Data Protection Principals

There are eight data protection principals:

1. Process personal data fairly and lawfully and shall not be processed unless:
    a. at least one of the conditions in Schedule 2 is met (see next section), and
    b. in the case of sensitive personal data, at least one of the conditions in Schedule 3 is also met (see consent section).
2. Obtain personal data only for one or more specified and lawful purposes and shall not be further processed in any manner incompatible with that purpose or those purposes.
3. Personal data shall be adequate, relevant and not excessive in relation to the purpose or purposes for which they are processed.
4. Personal data shall be correct and, where necessary, kept up to date.

5. Personal data processed for any purpose or purposes shall not be kept for longer than is necessary for that purpose or those purposes.
6. Personal data shall be processed in accordance with the rights of data subjects (individuals).
7. Appropriate technical and organisational measures shall be taken against unauthorised or unlawful processing of personal data and accidental loss or destruction of, or damage to, personal data.
8. Do not transfer personal data to a country or territory outside the European Economic Area unless that country or territory ensures an adequate level of protection for the rights and freedoms of data subjects in relation to the processing of personal data.

Frist Principal Conditions

Personal data should only be processed fairly and lawfully. For data to be classed as "fairly processed", at least one of these six conditions must apply to that data:

1. The data subject (the person whose data is stored) has consented ("given their permission") to the processing;
2. Processing is necessary for the performance of, or commencing, a contract;
3. Processing is required under a legal obligation (other than one stated in the contract);
4. Processing is necessary to protect the vital interests of the data subject;
5. Processing is necessary to carry out any public functions;
6. Processing is necessary to pursue the legitimate interests of the "data controller" or "third parties" (unless it could unjustifiably prejudice the interests of the data subject).

Consent Requirements

Except under these exceptions (National Security, Crime, Taxation and purely domestic purposes), the individual needs to consent to the collection of their personal information and its use in the purpose(s) in question. Additionally, consent should be appropriate to the age and capacity of the individual and the circumstances of the case. E.g., if an organisation "intends to continue to hold or use personal data after the relationship with the individual ends, then the consent should cover this." Plus, even when consent was given, it should not last forever.

Post-Brexit

It's expected that the DPA (or more likely its replacement) will change to continue as a more "free-standing" piece of UK legislation – the core concepts will remain the same. Although with the GDPR and the expected ongoing close ties to Europe that will remain, UK businesses will have to deal with both sets of regulations ongoing.

Australia – Privacy Act

The Australia Privacy Act 2000 extended the original Privacy Act 1988 to cover private sector organisations and businesses.

The act includes ten National Privacy Principles (NPPs) that regulate the collection, use, and disclosure of personal information. There is some flexibility in the interpretation, and the Federal Privacy Commissioner (FPC) make guidelines available to aid their interpretation. The FPC also has powers to investigate and resolve complaints made by individuals against organisations that do not follow the NPPs.

National Privacy Principles

The NPPS are:

1. **Collection** – what's collected, collecting from 3rd parties and telling individuals about the collection
2. **Use and Disclosure** – how organisations may use and disclosure individuals' personal information. If certain conditions are met, an organisation does not always need an individual's consent to use and disclose personal information. There are also rules about direct marketing.
3. **Information Quality** – take steps to ensure personal data is correct and up to date.
4. **Security** – personal data is secure from unauthorised use.

5. **Openness** – must have a policy on personal data management and make available to anyone who asks.
6. **Access and Correction** - individuals have a general right of access to their personal information, and the right to have it corrected if it's inaccurate, incomplete or out-of-date.
7. **Identifiers** – you're prevented from adopting an Australian Government identifier as your own.
8. **Anonymity** - where possible, give individuals the opportunity to do business with them without the individual having to identify themselves
9. **Transborder Data Flows** – how you should protect personal information transferred outside Australia.
10. **Sensitive Information** - Sensitive information includes information relating to health, racial or ethnic background, or criminal records. Higher standards are applied to the handling of sensitive information.

It's also interesting to note that the legislation protects the privacy of the dead up to 30 years after their death.

Mandatory Data Breach Reporting

As of 22nd February 2018, a business which:

- Has more than 3m AUD turnover since 2001, OR,
- Provides health services, OR,
- Trades in personal information, OR,
- Is a credit reporting body, OR,
- Is an employee association, OR,
- Provides services to the Commonwealth under a contract, OR,
- Operates a residential tenancy database, OR,
- Reports under the Anti-Money Laundering and Counter-Terrorism Financing Act 2006, OR,
- Conducts a protected action ballot

Needs to comply with the Mandatory Data Breach notification mechanism. Which requires a business to report hacks and leaks of personal data to customers if the breach causes "serious harm", examples of which (according to the Office of the Australian Information Commissioner (OAIC) guide) include:

- Financial fraud, including unauthorised credit cards transactions or credit fraud,
- Identity theft causing monetary loss or emotional and psychological harm,
- family violence, and,
- physical harm or intimidation.

Also, again from the guide, if a business is quick to act in remediating a data breach, and through this action, the data breach does not likely result in serious harm, there is no requirement to notify individuals or the commission. There is no specific definition of what 'quick' or 'remediate' means in this context.

Canada – Personal Information Protection and Electronic Documents Act (PIPEDA) and The Privacy Act.

In Canada what's considered personal data is broadly in keeping with our expectations and includes:

- Age, name, ID numbers, income, ethnic origin, or blood type.
- Opinions, evaluations, comments, social status, or disciplinary actions.
- Employee files, credit records, loan records, medical records, existence of a dispute between a consumer and merchant, intentions (e.g. to acquire goods or services, or change jobs).

Two pieces of federal legislation relate to privacy:

- **The Privacy Act** – covers how the federal government handles personal data;
- **Personal Information Protection and Electronic Documents Act (PIPEDA)** – covers how businesses handle personal data.

Personal Information Security & Systems Architecture

The Privacy Act relates to a person's right to access and correct personal data that the government holds about them in specific institutions[11]. Interestingly political parties and their representatives are exempt.

PIPEDA refers specifically to how private sector organisations collect, use and disclose personal data during for-profit commercial activities. It does not apply to the not-for-profit or charity groups, or political parties and associations.

PIPEDA at its core sets out ten principals[12] of fair information practices, as follows:

1. Be accountable
2. Identify the purpose
3. Obtain valid, informed consent
4. Limit collection
5. Limit use, disclosure and retention
6. Be accurate
7. Use appropriate safeguards
8. Be open
9. Give individuals access
10. Provide recourse

It's important to note that the Act contains an overriding obligation that any collection, use or disclosure of personal data must only be for purposes that a reasonable person would consider is appropriate in the circumstances.

To secure personal data under PIPEDA a business must:

- Develop and implement a security policy to protect personal data.
- Use appropriate security controls:
  - Physical measures: locked filing cabinets, restricting office access, alarm systems
  - Technological tools: passwords, encryption, firewalls
  - Organizational controls: security clearances, access via the "need-to-know" basis, staff training, agreements

---

[11] http://laws-lois.justice.gc.ca/eng/acts/P-21/page-11.html#h-35
[12] Privacy Toolkit for Business https://www.priv.gc.ca/media/2038/guide_org_e.pdf

- Regularly review security safeguards to ensure they are up-to-date and that known vulnerabilities addressed.
- Make employees aware of the importance of maintaining the security and confidentiality of personal information.
- Ensure staff awareness by holding regular staff training on security safeguards.

Strangely, at a Federal level, PIPEDA does not require personal data to remain in Canada, although provinces can overrule this.

Switzerland

Data protection regulation is by the Swiss Federal Data Protection Act (DPA) and the Data Protection Ordinance (DPO). The DPA contains:

- General rules on data protection.
- Regulations on data processing by private persons and federal authorities.
- Provision of the Federal Data Protection and Information Commissioner, the main supervisory authority.

The DPO explains certain features of the DPA provisions. In particular:

- Measures for the cross-border disclosure of data.
- Functions and duties of data protection officers and the Commissioner.

Before either creating personal data files at the federal level, or files that contain sensitive personal data, organisations & persons must register with the Commissioner (with a few exceptions around oversight, prior certification and journalism). In the case of transferring personal data abroad, specific requirements must be meet and, depending on the circumstances, inform the Commissioner prior to transfer.

Personal data processing must comply with the following general principles[13]:

- Personal data processing is only lawful (lawfulness).
- Personal data processing must occur in good faith and must be proportionate (proportionality).
- Personal data processing is only for the purpose given at the time of collection, evident from the circumstances, or that provided for by law (appropriateness).
- The collection of personal data and the purpose of processing must be evident to the data subject (transparency).

In addition, any person processing personal data confirms correctness and completeness[14]. Protection against unauthorised processing occurs by organisational and technical measures[15].

General exceptions from the DPA include:

- Personal data processed by natural persons just for personal use and not disclosed to third parties.
- Deliberations of the Federal Assembly and parliamentary committees.
- Pending civil and criminal proceedings, international mutual assistance proceedings and proceedings under the constitutional or administrative law, except for first instance administrative proceedings.
- Public registers based on private law.
- Personal data processed by the International Committee of the Red Cross.

Most Swiss cantons have enacted their own data protection laws regulating the processing of personal data by cantonal and municipal bodies.

---

[13] Article 4, Swiss Federal Data Protection Act (DPA)
[14] Article 5, DPA
[15] Article 7, DPA

To prepare for the EU GDPR, the Swiss parliament has issued a draft of a new Data Protection Act that:

- Modernises data protection law.
- Maintains the adequacy status granted by the European Commission, which ensures the free flow of personal data between the EU and Switzerland.

Its planned to introduce the new act by early 2019.

USA

Although the US doesn't have one single regulation that spans all states for general PII. There is at the federal level, under the Health Insurance Portability and Accountability Act (HIPAA)[16], defined the concept of Protected Health Information (PHI) which shares a lot of common data types as more general PII. PHI is:

- Names
- All geographical identifiers smaller than a state, except for the initial three digits of a zip code if, according to the current publicly available data from the U.S. Bureau of the Census: the geographic unit formed by combining all zip codes with the same three initial digits contains more than 20,000 people, and the initial three digits of a zip code for all such geographic units containing 20,000 or fewer people is changed to 000
- Dates (other than year) related directly to an individual
- Phone & Fax Numbers
- Email addresses
- Social Security numbers
- Medical record numbers
- Health insurance beneficiary numbers
- Account numbers
- Certificate/license numbers

---

[16] https://en.wikipedia.org/wiki/Health_Insurance_Portability_and_Accountability_Act

- Vehicle identifiers and serial numbers, including license plate numbers
- Device identifiers and serial numbers
- URLs & IP addresses
- Biometric identifiers, including finger, retinal and voice prints
- Full face photographic images and any comparable images
- Any other unique identifying number, characteristic, or code except the unique code assigned by the investigator to code the data

PHI applies to data collected when providing and paying for healthcare by a covered entity; such data is termed protected. Sharing of PHI with another entity requires the covered entity to ensure the third party has equivalent standards of privacy and confidentiality as themselves.

States

A trend to watch is individual states implementing tough PII and Privacy laws themselves. In June 2018 Arizona passed HB 2154[17] which implements:

- Maximum civil penalty per breach raised from $10,000 to $500,000.
- If a breach has occurred, notify the attorney general, as well as individuals affected within 45 days after discovery of the breach. If greater than one thousand affected, notify the consumer reporting agencies.
- Expanded definition of protected personal information (section 7, includes the username or e-mail address in combination with password or security question & answer).

Other states to implement similar bills include Orgon[18], Alabama[19], South Dakota[20], Vermont[21], Louisiana[22] and Colorado[23]. Some tougher than the Arizona legislation in terms of reporting requirements.

---

[17] https://www.azleg.gov/legtext/53leg/2r/bills/hb2154p.pdf
[18]   https://statescoop.com/oregon-gov-brown-considers-equifax-bill-to-protect-consumer-rights
[19]

Overarching Analysis

Given the range and scope of regulations in existence, there are a few high-level generalisations:

- A business collecting, processing, utilising or handing on personal information at some significant scale – it's highly likely they will need to comply to at least one PII regulation.
- Distinct types or classes of PII 'attract' differing regulatory treatments.
- Access to PII for an individual to verify, censure or correct is mostly universal.
- Security and integrity of PII is a common theme throughout all the regulations often with a mandatory breach disclosure requirement.
- Moving or accessing PII between different regulatory environments often requires specific treatment.

So, as a result, business will have to directly invest in improving how they treat PII in their systems, as well as invest in personal (or service providers) to see the treatment of PII is maintained over time. This also creates a strong incentive to 'fix' PII management just once and avoid expensive country by country (or states by state) tweaks.

Fair Information Practice Principles

Underpinning many of the PII and privacy regulations in force are a set of principles known as the Fair Information Practice Principles (FIPPs). These principles originally came from a US government committee to deal

---

http://alisondb.legislature.state.al.us/ALISON/SearchableInstruments/2018RS/PrintFil es/SB318-enr.pdf
20   https://privacy.huntonwilliamsblogs.com/wp-content/uploads/sites/18/2018/03/South_Dakota_SB62.pdf
21   https://legislature.vermont.gov/assets/Documents/2018/Docs/BILLS/H-0764/H-0764%20As%20Passed%20by%20Both%20House%20and%20Senate%20Official.pdf
22 https://www.legis.la.gov/legis/ViewDocument.aspx?d=1101149
23

https://leg.colorado.gov/sites/default/files/documents/2018A/bills/2018a_1128_signe d.pdf with the harmful consequences of using computer systems when processing data about individual citizens[24].

The principles are as follows:

- **Collection Information** – Do not collect more information than needed.
- **Data Quality** – You are responsible not to collect, store or use inaccurate data.
- **Purpose Specification** – Tell people why you want their data and get permission to use it as intended.
- **Use limitation** – Before using data you already have for a new purpose, you must explain why and get the appropriate permissions.
- **Security** – The data you hold is protected.
- **Openness** – be as transparent as possible to the people whose data is entrusted to you.
- **Individual Participation** – People should be able to see what you know about them and ask for the correction of mistakes.
- **Accountability** – you are liable for the responsible handling of the information.

If you look back through the regulations, you will see these core principals expressed.

Small Business

In the regulations, there are often exceptions for small businesses from having to comply or a reduction in the scope of compliance required. There are few things to note about this:

- There could well be other regulations in force on information processing that small businesses still need to comply with.

---

[24] U.S. Department of Health, Education and Welfare, Secretary's Advisory Committee on Automated Personal Data Systems, Records, Computers and the Rights of Citizens, 1973. Preface.

- The limits of what defines a small business (SMB) are often around turnover and staffing levels; a business could be in or out of scope across different legislation. For instance, the GDPR defines a small business as having less than 250 employees, whereas the Australian Privacy Act defines it by turnover of less than $3m AUD (with many exceptions[25]).
- Just because small business does not have to comply does not mean they do not need an approach to securing PII – something still needs doing as the risks remain.

In a similar vein, start-ups need to be incredibly careful how they approach regulations, as by definition start-ups will grow and often go beyond being small very quickly if successful. As a result, planning on regulations needs doing well in advance to avoid expensive mistakes and noncompliance issues.

Small businesses also need to be particularly careful if the GDPR applies to them, as the fine structure works on a percentage or fixed basis, whichever is the greater. The maximum fixed fine is €20m, which could easily sink a small business – so security and compliance are critical for a small business. A small business which is wilfully negligent in its approach to the GDPR could feel the full force of such a fine, whereas a business which was trying its best to comply would receive a fine proportionate (i.e. much smaller) and be able to survive a breach incident.

Key Points

- Many major economies and trading blocs have PII regulations in force (or about to come in force).
- PII needs specific treatment to follow these regulations over time.
- PII usage, storage, processing and who has access could well change because of having to comply.
- Distinct types of PII require different treatments.

---

[25]   https://www.oaic.gov.au/agencies-and-organisations/faqs-for-agencies-orgs/businesses/small-business

- There will be costs associated with compliance.
- Failure to comply is prohibitively expensive and can threaten the viability of a business.
- Plan well ahead to decide if a business needs to be compliant in the future. Revisit at least once a year.

Chapter 4
Business Investment Case

Any idiot can point out a problem ... A leader is willing to do something about it! Leaders solve problems!

Tony Robbins

Given the wave of PII regulations, it should be straightforward to get approval to make the required investment? Unfortunately, such investment is too often seen as a "naked cost" with no perceived market value. Which is akin to the classic problem in IT that nobody wants to invest until things start breaking badly, usually at this stage the costs to remediate the issue have ballooned as the chance for preventative investment have long gone.

What can an IT manager do to convince their management that investing in PII is something worth doing?

A way to present the arguments to invest are:

1. It's an added cost of doing business; failure to invest in PII regulation compliance isn't an option.
2. Likewise, all the competitors in the markets who manipulate similar PII 'should' be doing this as well.
3. Given PII regulatory compliance extends to the system to system (and hence business to business) relationships, not being compliant *will* result in lost business (a client can't use their business, they are precluded).
4. Therefore, given point #2 and point #3 above, *being PII compliant first gives a business a known market advantage.*
5. The PII compliance investment is made in such a way as to minimise ongoing costs of compliance and the costs of compliance in new markets. Which again provides a competitive advantage.

6. PII compliance investment also means the risks of doing business are reduced. As by its nature PII regulatory compliant systems are 'harder' to breach.

The core point is that the PII regulation needs the business to invest against specific PII security risks. It's an opportunity to differentiate and get ahead of the pack.

Also, such security investment can be part of a broader effort to more formalise the business security stance, for instance, ISO 27001 compliance could be a practical goal, something which can truly differentiate the business in the marketplace. Do be aware there can be significant initial compliance costs and then ongoing assessment costs; the return for investment case will need detailing.

Find a few PII data breach examples to show the business the scale of the problem and the potential costs incurred. Be careful not use them as a pure scare tactic, remember the expectation on the IT manager is to manage such risks, senior management should look to them to understand the risks. Use the breaches to provide an appropriate context that frames what to do regarding addressing real problems. Do not over-egg the risks, let the regulatory requirements lead. This approach should get the management buy-in.

Getting the Attention of Management

Now it may be that management does not want to hear a bar of it and consider the risks to be not worth investing against. In this case, gently point out the following:

- Quite a lot of the regulations permit both administrative fines and liability claims (in effect class actions for large-scale infringements);
- Some of the regulations allow imposing criminal sanctions;
- Some of the regulations can enforce a suspension in data processing on a business.

In short, the new wave of PII regulations has sharp teeth which can damage both a business and personal reputations (not to mention financial costs).

If management is still not interested, gently point out that they are now aware of their regulatory obligations and as such have chosen to disobey the law of the land. There is no excuse for business legal noncompliance.

If the management still disagrees to do anything on this matter, this could be a strong signal to look at working somewhere else; as there will be other problems getting IT critical investments made, and their inaction puts careers at risk. Sometimes this is the only possibility left.

PII Project Stages

At this stage, management should be wanting to know how to approach the project. The following projects stages are one practical way:

1. **PII Discovery & Analysis** – finding how PII is manipulated, where it's stored, who sees it, whom it's shared with and how its deleted. Then classifying the PII by type and country association. This will produce a PII Usage Report.
2. **PII Regulations Analysis** – given the types of PII data and its country associations, work out what regulations to follow (or must be complied with in the future based on business intentions). All delivered in a PII Regulations Report.
3. **PII Gap Analysis** – this is working out what to do, this can range from some simple system interfacing tweaks right up to a redesign of system architecture. The deliverable will be a PII Gap Analysis Report which also covers estimated timelines and resourcing needed for works approval and the order in which to approach the work.
4. **PII Works** – this is where all the changes occur to become compliant following the PII Gap Analysis.
5. **PII Resourcing** – This is where training, monitoring and reporting procedures are set up to support ongoing compliance needs. This 'embeds' compliance right into the business day to day.

Selling The Project To Your Staff

Now that permission was given, staff need to get on board, as on the face of it dealing with PII comes across initially as about as exciting as dealing with drying paint. Point out the following:

- The business must do this; it's a requirement of doing business when using PII;
- Processing PII correctly to follow the regulations can be challenging, there are techniques that will make the staff better at dealing with processing data in general.
- Data processing skills will improve, quite often looking at systems "data first" is a new experience for most systems and developer focussed people, it's assumed knowledge.
- The staff will get to understand most of the business and what people do, as PII will be all over the place. Therefore, a great networking opportunity.
- Working with PII & information security is a known skill in the marketplace. Therefore, doing this project improves personal 'worth'. It could take careers in a new and exciting path.
- The project is critical for the business, doing well in this project should have good career implications.

That should get them across the line.

Staff Skills Requirements

Working out the precise headcount needed will depend on the number of systems, how much will be done in-house and by when it needs doing. Although here are some pointers on hats that will need filling:

Data Architect

Someone whose job it is to find and keep track of where all the PII is, in particular:

- Where PII enters systems, what it is and who owns it (hint: this could have changed over time);
- Where PII sits in systems, what it is and who owns it;
- Which systems process PII.
- Where PII leaves systems, what it is and who then owns it and what rights of manipulation they have.

In effect, this individual or team knows 100% where your PII is always. They will also need to have a finger on the pulse of PII dependent projects to keep up to date on developments.

Data Analyst

Someone whose job is it to pop the hood on systems and go in to find where PII is, its quality and lifecycle. They should be competent technologists and able to work with many teams. You might be able to "flip this out" and get a senior engineer responsible for specific systems in another team to wear this hat on their systems behalf.

PII Regulations Guru

The PII Regulations Guru is the person who decides all the PII requirements. Such a person might be a consultant hired in as needed or could be someone who wears this hat part-time. Success in regulations compliance critically depends on this person. They must also be able to work with Architects and System owners to work out the proper treatment for PII – as it's possible through smart design and analysis to reduce the

PII surface and hence reduce the effort needed to comply (later). They should also be able to work with the legal team and point them in the right direction.

Senior Architect

Usually, this will be an existing Architect co-opted into the project to help ensure the required changes get implemented in a way consistent with system design best practices. They're respected within the business, suitably senior and able to get the required changes to the systems as needed.

Small Business and PII Compliance

At a small business, it's highly likely there will not be multiple layers of management to contend with to get things done, but there will be a lack of resources. There certainly will not be teams of people who can contribute to the effort.

In this case, a pragmatic and resource-constrained approach is proper, which revolves around assessing the most critical PII risks first. The PII and Data Analysis still needs doing, use an external consultant or agency to perform this; it all comes down to how many systems there are and who handles them. It could well be that the business uses completely Commercial Off the Shelf (COTS) software solutions, the business will still need to ascertain if they comply to the PII regulations on their behalf, which will require knowledge of what PII they hold.

Key Points

- Most businesses, even small to medium-sized businesses must assess their PII compliance requirements.
- If compliance is a requirement, the business must enact the regulations – ignorance isn't bliss.

- Noncompliance can result in fines, sanctions, suspension and even criminal proceedings!
- Depending on the business size and complexity they might need to set up a dedicated team or outsource the whole effort.
- Do not forget to cover cloud services and 3rd party integrations in PII discovery.

Chapter 5
PII Discovery

We seek him here, we seek him there,
Those Frenchies seek him everywhere.
Is he in heaven? - Is he in hell?
That damned, elusive Pimpernel?

Emma Orczy

Now it's time to do something constructive with the knowledge picked up in earlier chapters and start applying it to get to grips with PII. This chapter shows how to do PII Discovery or the *art* of finding where all PII is in the business.

It's an art for a good reason, as there is no one magic query to run across a database to show where PII is (or a document to pull out of the business archives). The knowledge of where PII is often sitting in that squidgy grey matter between people's ears – whats found from the systems will usually raise more questions than it answers. Have a look through the documentation, schemas, and code, but given a choice; ask people first as to where they think PII is. Just make sure they know what PII is first.

Privacy Impact Assessment

Such PII discovery is the first steps of a Privacy Impact Assessment (PIA), which is a way to help businesses identify the most effective techniques to comply with privacy and data protection regulations. A PIA is also an opportunity to identify PII processing problems early on and quickly reduce risks (covered in the next chapter).

Certain regulations (GDPR) require PIA's if performing the following 'high risk' processing:

- Systematic and automated PII processing, including profiling, if decisions produce legal effects or significantly affect the individual.
- Processing at a large scale of special categories of data (i.e. genetic or biometric data) or data relating to criminal convictions and offences.
- Systematic monitoring of a publicly accessible area on a large scale.

The GDPR also requires PIA's when implementing business changes, such as new products or systems that change personal data processing.

To aid in creating a PIA, open source software[1] is available for use by the Data Controller.

Prep work

First off, produce a complete business-wide diagram of all the software systems in use in a business. This also includes anything that could be "brought back to life" (Frankenstein's monster fashion) in an emergency, such as old code or systems with archived databases – as those databases could hold PII (many a hard drive has been thrown out by accident with sensitive data on it). It also includes systems planned on or possible to be used. Such an approach may sound all-embracing, but gaps cannot be afforded, it's critical to the success in managing the risks and compliance.

Most businesses have software systems relating to:

- Payroll / HR,
- Finance,
- Ordering and Inventory,
- Warehouse / Stock Management,
- Building Management,

---

[1]   https://www.cnil.fr/en/open-source-pia-software-helps-carry-out-data-protection-impact-assesment

- Fulfilment,
- Payment Processing,
- Mailing Lists/ Marketing,
- Websites,
- Customer Care,
- Support,
- Communications,
- Document Management,
- Customer Facing Services,
- Data Mining / Analytics / Reporting,
- Access Control / Security,
- Asset Management / System Operations,
- BCP / Backups

These *all* need checking.

It may be the case that diverse business units or regions, use different systems for the same system tasks – this multiplicity needs capturing. So, for a large business with a low level of centralized IT control, this initial prep work to get a diagram can be quite a chore (and management need to take this into account when scheduling). In such a situation it makes sense to have a diagram per region, even if there is overlap and sharing going on. What systems are in play needs seeing clearly and where the information flows, so do not risk something critical falling between the diagrams.

What's in the diagram

What needs to be in the diagram (and it can be a series of interconnected diagrams, don't cram everything into one) is the following:

- The diagram has two areas: "inside" the business (the business runs it and controls who accesses it) and "outside" the business (another business runs it, and it's accessed based on an arrangement). Put the outside to the top and inside to the bottom.
- Put in the outside section a box on each side called "Individuals" – PII flows from and to these people.

- Put in the outside section a box on each side called "businesses" – again PII flows to and from these businesses.
- For each system: its name, who provides it, its function (no more than three words) and an indication if it contains PII straight off based on its function (Yes / No / Maybe). Place the system either on the inside or outside. Then for each flow of data to and from that system put an arrowed line to or from the system or sink as needed.

Repeat this for all systems and data flows in the business. Try to set up the diagram so that data flows into the business from the left-hand side, then flows out on the right-hand side – this makes it much easier to see and trace data flows. It also means if by following the same diagram standard (up is outside, down is inside, left is earlier, and right is later) the diagrams will fit together much easier and won't cause nasty headaches trying to follow flows through many diagrams.

So, for example, say there is a set of systems that take in orders from the public and then ships those orders out as needed, dealing with everything in between, this could result in a diagram like that shown below.

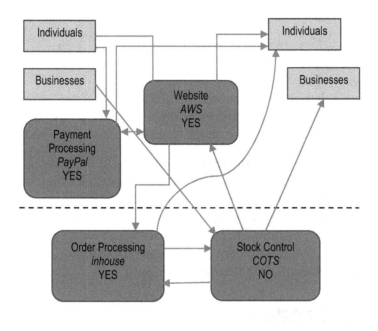

Figure 4 Simple System PII Dataflow

As you can see, for just these four systems, there a lot of data flows going on, and for at least 3 of the systems, there is high confidence that they contain PII from the start.

So, what does such a diagram tell you? First off, if there any systems that have no PII in them, and there is high confidence that this is the case – they can become "black boxes" – no need to know more about them. Although do a double check and confirm, PII has a habit of 'spreading'.

Secondly, it's highly likely to find clusters of PII exchange, such as between the Website, Order, and Payment processing systems shown in the diagram. Such clustering is a healthy thing to see as it shows:

- PII data is unlikely to be being manually re-entered or skipping systems via unknown data exchange.

- Therefore, less chance of data quality degrading as it flows through the systems.
- It's easier to secure such PII clusters than many disconnected systems.

Conversely, if there are lots of disconnected islands of PII all over the place, this either shows there is a missing system (or two) exchanging the PII for systems or missing data exchanges. Reinterview the key people and find out how the PII gets into those systems, even if it's by hand.

Start the diagramming from the most common PII data path and work out from there; so, if the business does the web-based ordering, start with the customer and the website and work outwards. Interview and perform information discovery on each system in turn. Don't expect to get it entirely right the first time, but the diagram will highlight quite easily where things do not look right in terms of the data exchanges. Quite often doing a quick draft diagram then sharing the diagram around can jog memories.

Where art tho Actors?

For those familiar with traditional data flow diagrams, all the Actors aren't in for three reasons:

- Who does/did what isn't that critical at this stage;
- Across multiple systems Actors tend to breed like Spring rabbits;
- Diagram space.

At this stage, it's important to see quickly where the PII is and who of external significance is interacting with it (we cannot directly control or check their usage). Shown later are the Actors to define PII access.

Other Places to Find PII

There are few other places where to find some PII lurking:

- **Website Access Logs** - parameters on requests could be in the access logs, so anything entered by a user could be there (this is a terrible security practice). The IP address of the accessing machine could also be PII under the EU GDPR regulations

- **Website Cookies** - it's not unheard of to embed key user details (like date of birth, age, etc.) into a cookie[2], to save having to keep looking it up.
- **API Tokens** - for a similar reason to the website cookies, this saves lookup time.
- **Temporary files** – look in program working directories and shared temporary directories for unused files holding PII.
- **Caching Frameworks** – these either are purely memory based or save to disc, the usual problem is it easy to gain access to them as a service.
- **IT Infrastructure** – Wi-Fi access logs, login records, machine MAC to IP address records, etc. Any mechanism that tracks individuals via their technology usage.

As shown above, PII can hang around in lots of hidden places. Be creative, do not be afraid to ask for people to step through in detail how they use PII and work out where it ends up going. This step is critical to working out how much remediation works needed and must be in depth and comprehensive.

Also, check to see how people enter PII into systems, are all the means of PII entry via computer to computer or does someone have to type in PII? If so, find out if this is entered directly, say from a customer care call, or is it entered off a printed form or note? Remember PII doesn't just have to exist on a computer, it can be on paper or other mediums.

Capturing Whole Data Flows

It could be that PII data flows have a rather 'varied' path through a business, they may start life as a telephone call recorded to an answering machine, which then gets transcribed onto paper and then at some point

---

[2] A piece of data for a website kept in website browser, so later that website can identify you using that browser.

put into a computer system. Such a path leaves a trial of physical PII, handled by many people, which needs managing in addition to what ends up in the computer system. Many regulations require specific management of such data flow paths to avoid PII becoming lost or misplaced (this is also why it is good to get PII into a secure computer system as soon as possible).

The previous diagramming technique won't capture the complete richness of such interactions, as its focus is on the computerised part of the process and the immediate touch points with physical processes and entity types. It won't capture standalone back-office processes that are highly manual.

In this case, it will be best to create a higher-level diagram to capture how PII physically gets into the computers systems (or out of them). Feel free to make use of a graphical format that is familiar to you[3], what you will need to capture is:

- The data lifecycle: where it comes from, where it's stored, where it's used, whom it's given to and how it's destroyed.
- The entities involved: the original data owner, the entity processing the data and any third parties who receive the data.
- The data formats: written, spoken, digital, email, media, documents, etc.
- The processing done and how data gets transferred around.
- Any boundaries as concerning jurisdiction, environment and physical geography (countries, regions, locations).

Use the first two items (life cycle and entities) to form a matrix into which the others are placed and then linked. With the data flowing from left (where it came from) to the right (destruction) and progressively down and out (to the third parties).

All data should have a complete flow from initial entry to final destruction (which may occur across multiple diagrams), if it doesn't either more discovery needs doing, or you have an incomplete or undefined data flow operating in the business.

---

[3] Flowchart symbols or AWS symbols https://aws.amazon.com/architecture/icons/

If you have many data flows to deal with, it could well become worth making use of data discovery and mapping tools[4] and documentation tools to keep on top of the mountain of information produced.

The benefit in capturing such flows is not only for awareness, but it could also bring to light data flows that are ripe for automation or complete removal.

Ethics

Something else to take into consideration is if the collection of PII in certain cases is ethical. It may not be in breach of any regulations, but it may be 'creepy' or big-brother by accident. Case to point, UNSW wound back the Wi-Fi data they collect as they were tracking toilet visits[5].

Its recommended using tools like The Ethics Canvas[6] to work out if the data collection is ethical or not. If something looks unethical note it down for later discussion.

Key Points

- PII discovery is finding out which systems could hold PII and the data flows in and out of those systems.
- For each system decide who runs it and if it's inside or outside of the business.
- Pay interest to flows to and from individuals and other businesses.
- Watch out for paper-based records.
- Determine if you need to capture in detail the physical PII data flows as well.

---

[4] Look for Data Flow Diagram Software and Threat Modelling Tools.
[5] https://www.itnews.com.au/news/unsw-winds-back-wi-fi-data-collection-on-staff-and-students-491357
[6] https://www.ethicscanvas.org/

Personal Information Security & Systems Architecture

- Consider if the collection of PII is ethical.

Chapter 6
PII Analysis

*The difference between something good and
something great is attention to detail*

Charles R. Swindoll

By this stage, there should be a good understanding where PII lives in the business systems, yet there is no knowledge of what form that PII takes and how much it's worth and hence what's at risk. This chapter explains how to do the analysis and what needs recording.

Assessing PII Value and Risks

To work out the value of PII in a system, look again at the qualities PII has as information, namely:

- Application
- Correctness
- Timeliness
- Uniqueness
- Relevance

(see the Information has value chapter for a description of these concepts)

The more correct, up to date, unique and relevant PII is the more its core value is to the business (and others). Such high-value PII, therefore, has a greater at-risk value to the business if it leaks.

For the sack of simplicity at this stage, let us assume all the PII is correct and relevant. Later, what to do with less accurate or complete PII gets covered.

PII differs in Value

Not all PII is equal, a person's date of birth is more private than their full name, but both get overshadowed by their tax file number. How are such differences reconciled to come to a unified understanding of PII value?

The pragmatic approach taken is to score each type of PII, the higher the score, the more "private" or valuable that PII is. In the table on the following page, is a 1 to 10 score for common types of PII (with 10 being the highest PII value). A brief description is also provided so that if there isn't an exact match, use the closest highest value PII type.

PII Type	Description	Value
Basic Name	Just First and Last (family) name	1
Full Name	First, Middle and Last (family) name	2
Face Picture	Clear picture of just the face	1
Face Picture with Geo Location	Clear picture of just the face associated with where it was taken	2
Picture with Identifier	Picture associated with who is in it	3
Plain Password	Password 'in the plain' or simple hash (Md5 hash without a salt for example)	6
Work Email address	Email for an individual at work	1
Home Email address	Email for an individual outside of work	2
Mobile Number	Personal Mobile Number	2
Home Number	Direct telephone of individual at home	2
Work Number	Direct telephone of individual at work	1
Home Address	Postal address of an individual's home	2
Work Address	Postal address where an individual works	1
Date of Birth	Full date of birth	4
Age	Age to a year or nearest month	1
Place of Birth	Where someone was born as on Passport or Birth Certificate	5
Social Security Number, Tax File Number, Passport Number, etc	Government issued individual ID number (can be a partial identifier)	10*
Sexual Preferences, Political Preferences	Personal Social Preferences	5
Gender	Individual's physical sex	3
Race, distinguishing features, height, weight	Body Characteristics	7
Mother's Maiden Name, First Pet Name, Street Grew up in, First Car, etc	Identity verification questions that depend on personal knowledge.	8
Bank Account Number	Financial Account Numbers	4
Provider Account Number	Service Provider Account Number (electricity, gas, etc.)	3
Medical Records, Legal Records, Police Records, Financial Records	Private & Personal records relating to aspects of life	10*
Eye scans, fingerprints, voice print, x-rays, facial features, etc	Biometric information either raw or encoded for matching	8*
Way paths, place visited, geodata, routes travelled, GSM tower logs, WIFI MAC logs	Where someone has been and when with date or time of day resolution.	6
Last accessed or logged into a system	System access records that record with date or time of day resolution.	3

Browsing History, Purchase Records, Search History	Records of activity online	5
Emails, 1to1 chats, etc	Private Correspondence	5

Table 1 - Values of distinct types of PII

Table Notes:

- Passwords are PII "by proxy" as the password might be reused across multiple systems and thereby facilitate identity theft. Its high value is due to password reuse being so common.
- Partial identifiers, say the first or last few digits of an ID, can be PII if they are sufficiently unique to an individual.
- Knowing what someone's first car was doesn't seem important – but often such innocent information (and an account number and address) are all that's between a cybercriminal and a customer care representative in business believing that the cybercriminal calling is a customer.

The above weightings are based upon several aspects, namely:

- The likelihood the information is already 'out there' and readily available to someone motivated to find.
- What could be done with the information if it got into the wrong hands.
- The legal and regulatory burden placed on that information.

For example, a person's name and date of birth are discoverable on Facebook if they made it visible (total score 5). Whereas if given someone's full name, their DOB, their home address and place of birth, that scores a total of 13. So such a score is mostly because the place of birth is hard to discover and used in identity theft (obtain the Birth Certificate and find where they live and get answers to ID validation questions, etc.).

It's important to note that for some types, like telephone numbers, the context of usage is essential. Mobile numbers can come and go with ease these days, whereas a home telephone number is more likely to be long-lived and therefore remain valid for longer.

Now, what about PII age? Are someone's financial records for the last year more valuable than their financial records from 5 years ago? One could argue the older financial records are less valuable, but financial records tend to hold other PII by implication, i.e. where someone has been at certain times, what they bought and from whom – that could enable *social engineering* to be done on a person or equally provide juicy material for the press.

> Social Engineering is where someone 'dupes' a person in a position of trust to reveal information they wouldn't otherwise do so using some social tricks and 'insider knowledge' to gain trust.

What about optional fields? Filling in the date of birth could be optional for example. In that case find out, as a percentage, how many times it's filled in. If the percentage is higher than 50%, count it as 100%. Use the percentage to adjust the value to the nearest rounded up integer (so in this example 50% of the records hold the date of birth, so the field score becomes 3). As for why the 50% limit on the adjustment, usually this indicates it was not optional and might be the result of a table merge instead or something historical (was mandatory in the past).

Sensitive PII

Some of the types of PII have a little star in the value column; this shows the PII type is very personally sensitive and often has "treatments" in legislation and regulations (often outside of pure PII legislation). Such PII is SPII (Sensitive PII) to make it clear it needs specific treatment beyond the more typical PII.

Having such SPII in a system can mean:

- The information gets stored distinct from other types of information.
- Requiring distinct methods of access control and monitoring.
- Audits and approvals needed <u>before</u> having such information in the systems.
- Periodic audits required while you have such information in the systems.
- Other regulations and legislation are complied with always, beyond the pure PII legislation.

If there is SPII in a system, it's best to do a quick check to see who has access to it and double check what systems handle it – it might have gone further than expected.

The Quantity of PII

The amount of a given set of PII also plays a part, although legislation often does not distinguish between having 5 records and 5 million – at the end of the day, the risks of losing 5 million is far greater than 5. This is due to the higher worth of 5 million records of known PII to cybercriminals, and therefore they are willing to spend far more effort obtaining compared to trying to copy just 5 records. As the old saying goes: Quantity has a quality all its own.

The sheer density of the number of records stored also creates its own modern-day logistic management problems. For instance, it's easy to misplace millions of records on a small Terabyte hard drive. The physical dimensions of information storage in no way indicates the value or volume held. A 50Mb hard drive not long ago was the size of a shoe box and before that a fridge. Therefore, sensitive information keeps turning up on laptops and thumb drives.

Yet equally, 5 million records are not a million times more valuable than 5 records, the relationship isn't linear, just because there is a multiple more of PII does not make it worth that multiple more to a cybercriminal. The risks associated with obtaining such data could be off-putting plus volume is no guarantee on its own of quality. Also, remember those who have millions or billions of PII are either large businesses or nation-states; they can afford to be secure and should be.

So how is this accounted for in comparing value? Just count the number of digits in the number of records and multiplying that by the score per record to get a score per table. So, for example, as above, if a record scored 13 for 10 million records, the total score is 104 (13 times 8). If a record contains SPII, this needs flagging as well.

A good technique is to roll all this up in a table for quick reference, for example.

Table Name	Customer	Mailing List	Employees
Record Score	13	3	23
#Record	10,000,000	50,000	500
Final Score	104	15	69
SPII?	No	No	Yes

Table 2 - Example PII Table Scoring

What does the Final Score Indicate?

The final score shows the "desirability" or raw worth of that table of information to a cybercriminal. The higher the score, the more desirable that table is to hack and the more considerable efforts a cybercriminal (or insider) will go to obtaining it. The score is therefore also an indication of the confidentiality (in a CIA[1] sense) of such information, as highly confidential information is highly valuable to a cybercriminal by default.

Therefore, you can consider it a sign of what effort to expend in protecting such information compared to other PII containing tables within the systems. Do not forget about the other PII; it will still need protection under PII regulations. Rather, the score helps in decision making on what must be dealt with first, and the effort spent securing it. Also, do not forget about other information that is not PII that has high worth, they too need a proper degree of protection.

Also look at those tables holding SPII – these will often need specific dedicated treatment and techniques that would be appropriate to the most highly scored PII (see the PII Vault Chapter later). As shown in the table above, a Customer table carries the highest final score, yet there is an internal Employees table that contains SPII (tax file numbers). The Mailing List in comparison isn't worth looking at yet; likely the cybercriminals

---

[1] CIA – Confidentiality, Integrity and Availability – the triad of security qualities and certainly not the USA government department of the same name (see later).

already have that from someone else (just not a list specific to this business).

To aid in efficiently working through this process, a worksheet is available at https://www.aykira.com.au/books/ .

Ranking The PII Per System

Having done the scoring given in the earlier section, you should have a set of final score tables, one per system. To compare across systems, create a table with columns for system name, location, highest scoring table, the total score for all tables and SPII, as follows:

System Name	Location	Highest Score	Total Score	SPII
Customer	Inside	104	119	No
HR	Outside	69	69	Yes
Financial	Inside	40	95	Yes

Table 3 - PII Score per System

The beauty of such a table is it's clear that:

- The respective distribution of PII not only within a single system but across all systems. This way it's clear if a specific table is pulling a system into PII compliance or it's just a consequence of what a system does.
- Where the most value rests across all the systems, regardless of size.
- What systems require specific SPII treatment are clearly visible.
- What systems outside of the immediate business control are holding PII on its behalf.

- The fit between the function of a system and the amount of PII held or processed by it.

Such a table is handy for communicating findings to management; it condenses the analysis down into something readily understandable. In the above table, for instance, the HR system could be a potential PII risk, as it's an external system holding SPII related to the employees; examine this as a priority (more on this later).

An improvement to help management understand the table is to rebase everything to scale to be out of a 100 per column so that the above table would become.

System Name	Location	Highest Score	Total Score	SPII
Customer	Inside	100	100	No
HR	Outside	66	57	Yes
Financial	Inside	38	79	Yes

Table 4 - Collated PII System Scores

With such a table it's clear the Customer information in total has getting on for double the value of the HR information without doing any mental maths. It can also be seen that the Financial system has lots of PII in various places, compared to those systems with the most PII.

Defining the Actors

Now it's time to find out who is accessing the various PII containing systems, given the understanding of the value and volume of information at their fingertips.

For each system go back to those responsible and ask the following questions:

- Who, as in individual or as a role, has access to PII or the technology holding the PII?
- What can they do once they have access?
- Are they an employee, contractor or another party?
- How do you identify who is accessing your system?

Try to keep the Actor titles short and as specific and descriptive as possible and then follow the name with their employment status, for example:

- System Admin (Employee),
- Data Entry Clerk (Contractor),
- Customer Care (Employee),
- Data Mining Agency (Business)

Yes, a business can be an Actor, for instance, the Data Mining Agency could be copying out PII via an API – this is just an automated action rather than a person doing it by hand. Pick up such data transfers from the original system diagrams, which were external businesses included at that stage.

Also, if the Actor is the same across different systems use the same name, whenever referenced highlight the name in **bold**. These are Actors who span multiple systems, so have a view into lots of otherwise disconnected PII. Such actors are essential to highlight, as the risks of accidental or deliberate exposure are higher.

At the end of this, there should be a card per Actor that details their key information based on the questions. Which also a good point to jot down anything which did not make sense and needs further resolving; especially if there isn't a clear understanding of what each Actor can do (create, modify, view, export/dump or destroy) with the PII.

Outsourcing

Something to aware of is when outsourcing functions to another business which runs in another country – usually for call centre / customer care / support / development type services. On paper it might look like they are full-time employees of the business, to even being in the HR system, but behind the scenes is an outsourcing arrangement with a 3rd party business which manages the engagement locally. Such employees are external for PII – as there are often specific regulations about accessing PII across the international country or regional boundaries to respect.

Where do Contractors and Consultants Sit?

One could argue a contractor is both internal and external. On the one hand, they could be remotely working for multiple clients at the same time which are external to the business. Equally, they could be a consultant embedded into the business to fill a need and are well known to staff internally.

The decision made usually comes down to the function performed, the way in which its enacted, and the professionalism (reputation and integrity). Evident and proven trust is a factor in this.

Once done there should be up to a dozen or so Actors; less than three it's highly likely people were missed (someone to maintain, someone to enter and someone to use. If they are all the same person, this could be a problem!).

Collating the Actors

There are several useful views into the Actors per system that to help understand their interaction with PII and the risks entailed.

External/Technical Risk Map

There should be a mix of Actors who map into one of four quadrants in the diagram below:

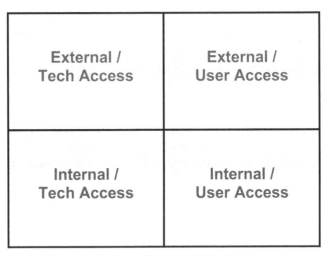

External / Tech Access	External / User Access
Internal / Tech Access	Internal / User Access

Figure 5 - External/Technical Risk Map

Based on whether they have access to the technology of the system (developers, devops, admin, etc.) or if they are external or not to the business.

What should be of concern at this stage is if there are any Actors in the top two boxes. If so, data is being manipulated or maintained by third parties over which the business has no direct authority or low visibility.

Means of Authentication List

In security terms, authentication is the act of identifying whom someone is using a challenge and response. Most people encounter this with the traditional username and password login forms, where both the username and password need to be correct (specifically the password matches the one stored for that account username).

> BTW **never** store passwords "in the plain", use a long & salted hash at least. No authentication service should 'know' directly what makes it authenticate or it could just be extracted by a cybercriminal and used against it.

What's covered here is what different authentication services or mechanisms are in play to decide who is who, and if the method used is appropriate to the access given.

It could be the system only has one global service that does this for all systems, or there could be many different mechanisms that give authentication. For instance, data entry clerks may use a traditional username and password, while the people who look after the technology implementing the system use something completely different (long-lived token-based login perhaps?).

To create the list, provide a headline per authentication service (with who is providing that service) and then list under each heading the Actors who use that means of authentication. For example:

Username and Password

3rd party OAuth service
Data Entry Clerks
Customer Care

SSH public key

Operating System
System Admins

Username and Password

Database Service
Database Admin

From the above list is it easy to see that the Database Admin has the same type of authentication method (not with the same usernames and passwords) yet has a much greater scope of access.

It's also clear that three of the Actors are in bold, this means they have access to the same role to PII in other systems, potentially using the same authentication mechanisms. See how quickly it highlights areas for investigation, as it cuts across different systems by the people who interact with them; this is a view rarely explored.

Types of Authentication

Although not an exhaustive list, these are the typical ways to achieve authentication:

- **Physical:**
    - o Key
    - o PIN code or Combination
    - o PAC card or RFID tab
- **Biometric**
    - o Thumbprint
    - o Handprint
    - o Facial scan
    - o Retinal / Iris Scanner
- **Logical**
    - o Username and password
    - o Username and one-time token generator
    - o Long-lived token or key
    - o Location or network address

Depending on the security context, it's possible to find that two or more of these techniques get combined, known as 2 to 3 Factor Authentication[2] (2FA & 3FA) or Multifactor Authentication (MFA). For instance, online banking usually requires 2-factor with some ID number, a password, and a one-shot token to log on. Some take this even further and require the use of a credit card with the token generator & PIN, in effect making it a stronger 2-factor (something you know with 2 things you have, one you keep on you, one you usually don't).

---

[2] For a stricter definition, see Authentication in Chapter 7.

From this can be concluded that roles which cut across PII containing systems and have a high degree of access, need additional factors of authentication over less 'privileged' roles. So, from the above example list, the Database Admin uses Username and Password for access directly to the database, the same level of authentication as a lowly Data Entry clerk! Such a situation can occur if not paying attention to restricting database access. Cybercriminals will scan for such oversights, to them such Privileged Accounts make an ideal target. Ideally, such low-level database access should be at least 2-factor if not 3 and locked down to requiring access via a bastion host (security hardened machine via which admin access to other services occurs, 'bouncing' via that server).

Bringing It All Together

At the end of this the following PII details are available:

- **How systems exchange PII** – the System PII Dataflow diagrams
- **The PII held in each table per system** – the per table PII score tables
- **The ranking of the PII value per system** – the PII system rankings table.
- **Internal / External Actor access** – the External / Technical Risk Map
- **How Actors are Authenticated** – the Means of Authentication List

Initial Risk Checks

At this stage, it's good to ascertain if the handling of PII is up to a minimum safe level – in that there isn't something wrong going on. Such a quick sanity check is done as follows:

1. Print out the PII System Rankings Table, the Internal / Technical Risk Map and the Means of Authentication List.
2. Using a highlighter pen (we suggest coloured Red) on the PII System Rankings Table and mark any row that has SPII set to Yes

– this is PII that needs treatment in own right under specific regulations, it needs keeping apart from anything else. To this end:

    a. Look at the Means of Authentication Lists for the highlighted Systems; any roles turn up in bold shared with other none SPII systems? If so there is a potential *Shared Role Leak* (a PII anti-pattern, see later) – mark Red and make a note.

    b. Look at the External/Technical Risk Map for the highlighted Systems; any Roles bolded turning up the External boxes? If so there is a potential *External Access Problem* (a PII Anti-pattern, see later) – mark Red and make a note.

3. On the same PII Systems Rankings Table, look for none SPII rows whose High Score is over 60; these are systems with a single block of high-value PII within them.

    a. Again, look for roles that are bold in the Means of Authentication List for these systems – a potential Shared Role Leak, mark in Amber and make a Note.

    b. Look at the External/Technical Risk Map for the highlighted Systems; any Roles bolded turning up the External boxes? They are a potential External Access Problem, mark them in Amber and make a Note.

At the end of this should be one the following four situations:

- **No red or amber highlighting** – success, PII that needs keeping apart is, and a basic level of distinct access control is evident.
- **Just Red** – indicating potential access to SPII via shared or external Roles across Systems.
- **Just Amber** – indicating potential access to high-value PII via shared or external Roles across Systems.
- **Red and Amber** – lots of shared or external Roles with mixed access to both SPII and high-value PII, this is a grave issue.

Remember, at this stage; it's not about security standards, technologies or processes, this is about understanding who has access to what as the business is currently set up and therefore whose best placed to commit a significant breach and get away with it.

If there are any Amber or Red, check:

- Who fulfils the highlighted Roles? Is it an individual, a team or an external agency?
- Are there any controls in place to log PII access? For instance, when someone logged in as the Role and what they did? Are logins shared?
- Are there mechanisms available for someone in that role to 'dump' records on mass to file? Could be simple as Print Screen to PDF if they can list all the PII records on one screen, or the ability to save a web-based report to a file. Or the app itself allows the export (wouldn't be the 1st time).

If there is either no consistent logging or a dump to file mechanism is evident – this means someone in that Role could copy out all the PII and nobody would be the wiser. This situation needs <u>immediate</u> remediation as a priority. Also, check if anybody left the Role and was locked out correctly by updated access controls.

<u>Confidentiality Risk Impact Level</u>

To make it easier to assign the proper security controls to the PII value and hence risk, assign to each system a Confidentiality Risk Impact Level of either High, Medium or Low as follows:

- **High** - contains SPII or has a High Score over 60 or has Red or Amber highlighted roles.
- **Medium** – has a Total Score over 60.
- **Low** – everything else.

So, from the example Systems Table, repeated below:

System Name	Location	Highest Score	Total Score	SPII
Customer	Inside	104	119	No
HR	Outside	69	69	Yes
Financial	Inside	40	95	Yes

The three systems are all rated as High by these rules.

This analysis may be overkill, but go back and look at the PII, its value and how it's accessed. The risks are there and proportional to the information.

For the sake of argument, say there was a System missed, the Access Control System to the head office, and it had the following PII Score table:

Table Name	Account	Card	Access Log	Roles Map
Record Score	4	3	3	0
#Record	5	1,000	50,000	500
Final Score	4	12	15	0
SPII?	No	No	No	No

This system has a High Score of 15 and a total of 31 with no SPII or shared or external roles. This business controls the system and knows who is responsible for it.   On that basis, the system is assigned a Low Confidentiality Risk Impact Level.

Now, on the face of it, assigning a Low-Risk level to what's a core piece of physical Access Control for staff and hence security infrastructure seems counter-intuitive, but this is just looking at systems through a lens that focusses purely on the PII aspects; ignoring what else they do for the business. It could be, as in this case, more security controls must be in place, but they are beyond this remit if focusing on the PII risks alone.

Tying into a Security Risk Analysis

Depending on the size of organisation, an existing risk assessment methodology could be in place. The results of this PII value and Risk impact analysis would feed into both the impact and likelihood of threat analysis stages by form a highest risk/probably 'union', in that the highest risks or likelihood 'wins' for consideration; given the cybercriminal motivation to obtain PII is an independent factor.

This is a crucial point to take on board, evaluation of risks must always include what external parties consider of value. As this will directly determine the reward and hence motivation undertaken by an external bad actor. Just because something is seen as low value to a business does not mean it won't have a higher value in another context.

Key Points

- Determine the value of PII to the cybercriminal to decide the risk and hence controls required to protect it.
- Distinct types of PII have different values.
- Certain sensitive types of PII needs specific regulatory treatment.
- The quantity of PII you have contributes to its value.
- Determine a PII value score per table of PII. Then total per system.
- Whom the actors are accessing the systems needs working out. Watch out for external actors and roles or logins shared across systems.
- Check the method of authentication is appropriate to the degree of access.
- Check if there is a Shared Role Leak or an External Access Problem and remediate.
- Uses the scoring and the presence of SPII to decide the confidentiality risk impact level. Double check all systems are assessed.

Chapter 7
Core Information Security Principles

For me, privacy and security are really important. We think about it in terms of both: You can't have privacy without security.

Larry Page

Before exploring the security aspects around PII, it's essential to take a step back and cover some core security principles, to ground our understanding and make sure a standard terminology is shared.

Those familiar with IT security can safely skip this Chapter, although it might do some good to have a quick refresher.

CIA

No, this isn't referring to a certain USA government agency, in this context CIA stands for Confidentiality, Integrity, and Availability of data. Information Security strives to balance these three qualities while keeping a focus on efficient policy implementation (so a business does not disappear under a mountain of red security tape).

But what does CIA mean? It helps to look at each of the words in turn:

- **Confidentiality**– information that needs keeping secret remains so and accessed by those only authorised to do so.
- **Integrity** – information as stored stays intact and isn't corrupted.
- **Availability** – those who need to have access to the information can do so when required. Which protects legitimation users against

deliberate attacks on systems that make them unavailable or 'acts of god' that would otherwise disable a service.

So, in short, CIA is about keeping safe and intact information for those who require access to it, without overburdening the business who must do this.

Typically, CIA gets implemented in a business via a risk management process which operates as follows:

1. Determine the assets of the business and their worth;
2. Determine the threat sources to the business, in effect whom could do them harm;
3. Discover the vulnerabilities that could cause harm to the business assets and the possible impacts;
4. Work out and implement what controls could minimise the risks to the business assets going forwards;
5. Assess the actual effectiveness of the Risk Management Plan as enacted above.

Now, this is all fine and dandy on paper, but in a genuine business applying CIA principals and all that entails can be a struggle; especially when applying to a business that has not had an information security ethos or mindset before.

CIA in Use

In practice CIA is a very high-level concept, it needs mapping down into the business information infrastructure via three primary areas:

- **Communications** – how information exchanges between systems and when it's allowed
- **Hardware** – the physical security of the equipment the systems and services run on.
- **Software** – the software itself needs securing.

These three on their own are not enough; they focus on the pure information security aspects. Around these are three further layers:

- **Physical** – security measures associated with the physical environment
- **Personal** – security measures that relate to the individual
- **Organisational** – Procedures and policies used to enact information security using the available services.

In this way, Information Security embeds into a business as part of "business as usual" and thereby ensuring ongoing security by the careful application, audit and ongoing review of processes and procedures. Key to this is a periodic Risk Assessment.

Risk Assessment

The risk assessment is performed by a dedicated team of domain knowledge experts with the help of various key people throughout the business. The risks relate to the risk of harm (or loss) of an information asset via a security vulnerability and how likely that threat is to occur (to quantify the risk). The impact of a threat as enacted also needs assessing to work out the real damage done, and the full costs incurred. Only then can risk and its consequences to a business be understood fully, and security controls deployed to mitigate the risks (or it decided to do nothing if the costs of mitigation are more significant than the damage costs).

According to ISO 27002, it recommends examining during a risk assessment:

- **Security Policy** – what specific security policies are in place, how they get enacted and kept up to date;
- **Organization of Information Security** – are specific people responsible for Information Security and do they have the resources to enact that responsibility;
- **Asset Management** – are assets tracked, catalogued and understood;
- **Human Resources Security** – are roles & responsibilities adequately matched to personnel, are sufficient vetting and screening checks in place, are confidentiality agreements in place;

- **Physical and Environmental Security** - do alarms & CCTV work, are doors locked, are visitors escorted, is there zoning and access control in place and is it logged;
- **Communications and Operations Management** - clear paths of communication and escalation procedures;
- **Access Control** – standardised and uniform control over access to assets and systems, with timeouts and lockouts and session-based controls.
- **Information Systems Acquisition, Development and Maintenance** - Configuration and set up ensuring correct operation of security controls;
- **Business Continuity Management** - plans, procedures, and systems in place to deal with accidents or outages.
- **Regulatory Compliance** – awareness of regulatory environment and processes and procedures to enforce compliance.

All the work done in analysing the information risks in the business boil down into a report that focusses on two things: assets and risks.

The assets will usually be a list of assets with their type, who owns it and any comments. Whereas the risks will look at each asset in turn and assess the criticality (in an information security sense, remember CIA) against the threats, their likelihood of occurrence, what controls manage the risk and if that is acceptable.

Risk Treatments

From the risk assessment report will come a list of risk remediation recommendations for management to enact as needed. Usually ordered by decreasing criticality. They come in four types:

- **Risk Avoidance** – this is the complete removal of the exposure to a given risk.
- **Risk Transfer** – giving the risk to another entity (for instance by outsourcing or putting in place insurance).
- **Risk Acceptance** – the business is happy to take on the risk as is.
- **Risk Mitigation** – apply techniques to reduce damage costs or likelihood (or both) of the specific risk.

The treatments used depends on the capabilities of the business and their appetite (or dislike) for the risks as presented.

Threat Modelling

It's usual during a risk assessment that a whole shopping list of potential threats and gaps are collated. The questions that come from this include:

- Is this all the possible threats?
- Which are prioritise first?

Threat modelling attempts to answer these questions by using a systematic analysis of the attacker (cybercriminal), the attack vectors and the assets attacked.

Most threat modelling occurs by a careful examination of the systems in question by security domain experts who have an in-depth understanding of how cybercriminals operate, and the common ways systems become compromised.

There have been many attempts to better formalise the process of threat modelling, from card games[1] that prompt considering varied attack scenarios through to full formalised methodologies[2]. Each suffers from the same problem, in that the threat surface does not stand still, so if not updated continuously 'blind spots' in the threat coverage and assessment can be created. So, to get adequate coverage, be aware of the latest attack vectors in favour and double check assumptions.

Also, remember when looking at how to respond to a given attack vector, there are four options:

- **Defend as is** – add-on security controls at a specific system or service;
- **Push deeper** – move the system or service under threat deeper into the architecture, so it's no longer able to be under threat;
- **Merge into** – recode the system or service to be part of an existing system or service with better security controls.

---

[1] https://www.owasp.org/index.php/OWASP_Cornucopia
[2] https://www.owasp.org/index.php/Threat_Risk_Modeling

- **Disable** – it may not be possible to get the degree of security required in the timeframe available. Therefore disable the system or service at risk for its own safety. This option is a last resort as it can often have a direct business impact.

Most usually go for the first option – but the three other options are just as valid in their approach, the outcome is the same in a security sense. This is where you get an interplay between system architectural and security concerns. The architecture of systems and services broadly define the security surface and the options available.

Security Controls

Security Controls are how a risk or threat gets managed to reduce the likelihood of its occurrence and hence the cost to the business.

Such security controls are split into three groups:

- **Administrative Controls** – these are all the policies, procedures, standards and guidelines that are followed when running the business. Such controls are required by law or required by a specific business sector (PCI DSS and Health for example).
- **Logical Controls** – these are the technology-based controls over access to data and the monitoring of that access. Think of it as the controls built into the system software.
- **Physical Controls** – these control and monitor access to the workplace and where and how information gets processed. They place appropriate restrictions and protections to ensure the ongoing security of operations.

Separation of Duties

One of the goals of the risk assessment is discovering people (and processes or systems) that operate in isolation without sufficient checks and balances to ensure security. For instance, it may be that an employee can submit a request for reimbursement and be able to authorise the payment all on their own– this could be open to abuse, so some third-party needs introducing to the process to 'separate' the combined duties and reduce the likelihood of abuse.

Equivalently, a database administrator could be writing payment processing code, these two roles and responsibilities should not rest with the same person. They either need splitting, or a third party introduced to give independent quality control.

From these two examples, you will see how crucial independent monitoring is to the security effort. It acts as a capable guard against most forms of process or system abuse.

Defence In Depth

Defence in depth (or Defence by Depth) is a technique of using multiple overlapping Security Controls to protect an asset. The idea being it's tough to successfully defeat all the controls in place and gain access to the asset.

Given information is either at rest or on the move between different systems we need to ensure that security controls are in place no matter where the information goes. By using multiple controls at once, we guard against a single weakness or failure critically affecting our ability to protect our information – it gives our implementation of security a high degree of built-in resilience against both attacks and unforeseen changes. Changes are a common cause of breakdowns in security coverage, so much so that organisations have specific processes to deal with change (see later) and reduce the risks.

Such a defence by depth approach can not only be within a single environment it can also be across the Administrative, Logical and Physical Controls as well. For instance, a secure server room has processes around signing in and out, PAC controlled doors, security cameras, alarms, physical machine rack locks and even admin passwords and encrypted drives that all work together to provide layers of security around the asset (the server and its information).

Information Classification

It's vital in information security to understand the actual value of the information within a business and therefore what are the proper ways to protect such information. The chapter on Information Analysis examined in detail what the true value of information is and discussed that information has at least two sources of value, what the business thinks its value is and what a cybercriminal thinks its value is, they need not be the same.

To this end, Information Classification (also confusingly called Data Classification) seeks to give information a security classification, by which it can be categorised and appropriately protect the different information in systems. A policy document defines the classification scheme that decides the labels assigned, what the criteria are for assigning a label and the resultant security controls that need enacting per label. Depending on the needs of the business and the type of information in play there could be anywhere up to six or more different classifications.

For such an information classification policy to efficiently work all staff need training in its application and how to approach each different type of classification.

Access Controls

Only those allowed access should see and manipulate information. Access Control is the mechanism which enforces such access. Those who need access must pass through three steps successfully: identification, authentication, and authorisation.

Identification

Identification is when someone (or something, like a program) asserts as to whom it is. In most computer systems this is a username or email address specific to the individual in question. But before they can access the secure information, they will need to verify they are indeed that person.

Authentication (AUTHN)

Authentication is the act of verifying the claim of identity. Which uses some information only that specific individual would know or some action or attribute only that individual can have. In this way authentication uses three types of information:

- *Something they know*: a password, PIN, or secret answer
- *Something they have*: driving licence, passport, PAC card
- *Something they are*: biometrics such as fingerprints and voice prints.

If multiple types of authentication get combined, then you have two-factor (2FA) or multiple factor authentication (MFA), also termed as strong authentication. Authentication can also be classified as being active or passive (Eiji Hayashi, 2013).

Authorisation (AUTHZ)

Once a person has been successfully identified, we then need to determine what they're permitted to do with the information sources. This process is called authorisation.

Strong authorisation depends on sound administrative policies and procedures used as the basis of the computer systems configuration.

Implementation of access control uses three mechanisms:

- **Non-discretionary** – all access control is under one central service. Access to information is determined centrally by role and tasks to be performed.
- **Discretionary** – the creator or owner of the information resource controls who has access.
- **Mandatory** – access is controlled via the security classification assigned to the information resource.

The Need -to-know Principle

An important principle is that a person gets access to exactly what they need to perform their job function and no more – hence the need-to-know. If they cannot prove they need to know they do not get access and it remains confidential (in a CIA sense). This principle stops *access overreach* whereby someone gets to see something they should not due to sloppy or ill-defined access controls.

This will often turn up by people having so-called Privileged Accounts when they do not need them, for instance:

- Board or senior management level staff having administrative access or 'see all' access to systems;
- Systems Administrators with admin access to everything regardless of where deployed and function.

In such cases access either needs revoking, restricting or making dependent upon two individuals to enact (split multifactor in effect).

Monitoring

An important part of maintaining security is having in place a reliable and provable alerting and monitoring framework. So, if a breach occurs its rapidly detected and dealt with.

This is where SIEM (Security Information and Event Management) frameworks collect logs and events from a variety of systems throughout a business to provide a unified view of the operational security state of the IT systems.

Insider Detection

A growing vector for data breaches is the actions of a bad actor insider who has privileged access to systems and information. This is of concern given the variety of computing systems and services used in a modern business and the multitude of ways of accessing those systems (BYOD, VPN, smartphones, work from home, etc.).

The bad actor could be an employee who is:

- Underperforming and disgruntled;
- About to leave for another business;
- Under duress.

They could also be suffering from identity theft or access credential theft (their machine might have a backdoor on it) and be completely innocent.

In response to this technology is developing (mostly based off marketing research techniques) to digitally 'profile' employees as they go about their day to day work – the aim being to detect quickly when their activities become suspicious or they 'rogue'. This is known as User and Entity Behaviour Analysis (UEBA).

Identity Analysis

To perform such an analysis, an additional level of detailed event logging needs undertaking to cover off all work actions (such as system accesses, document manipulations, printing, scanning, physical movements, etc.). This can then lead to a more dynamic approach to identity and access management that can keep pace with the evolving workplace needs and always maintain the right level of access. For instance, the process of dealing with: excess access, shared high privileged accounts and dormant accounts can be automated. This dynamic and automated approach to identities and access management is known as Identity Analytics (IdA).

Zero Trust Networks

Now the previously mentioned Defence in Depth technique has a lot going for it, but it's dependent upon how well partitioned the services are to preserve security in the face of a horizontal attack. For instance, see the network services set out below.

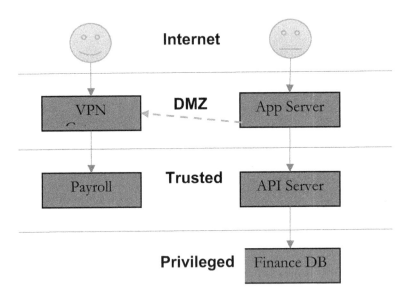

Figure 6 - Layered Network Security

In this, the least trusted environment is at the top, and most trusted at the bottom. Traffic to get from one layer to another must go through a service to get to a lower more trusted service. The problem with this is a lateral attack; if the App Server gets compromised, a cybercriminal could move laterally (the dotted line) to then attack the VPN gateway in the same DMZ network segment. Also, there is tendency the deeper into the trust layers; communications become more trusted so that a lateral attack can have a higher likelihood of success. Then if it's considered that such trust layering is just one view into the way services are organised, and you soon realise that unless there is perfect control and awareness 24 / 7 over what's going on, there will always be a risk of lateral attack.

The answer to this rat's nest of interplays between systems is not to have any division of trust, instead treat each system as its own 'island' and set up the service as if it was on the public internet and exposed to all and sundry. The idea here is that the ability of the cybercriminal to move between different services is curtailed by having to prove identity and authorisation for each system, the trust isn't 'transitive'.

The Zero Trust model (Gilman, 2017) turns the assignment of trust between services into a case by case assignment. Instead of the hierarchy of network segments, everything starts out not trusting anything else and being in their own islands. It's up to a new service, known as the Control Plane to decide what can talk to what.

In effect, each service acts as if it was within the least trusted environment, the Internet, and the Control Plane decides what communication between systems and services can occur. So, given the above network services, in the Zero Trust Network model, we end up with the following diagram.

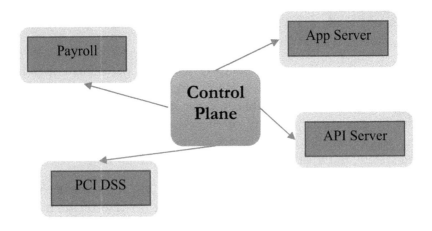

Figure 7 - Zero Trust Networking Example

In this diagram, surrounding each service is a red halo of access control, and by default this halo blocks everything. How such access control gets implemented often builds on firewall services built into modern operating systems, plus networking infrastructure (such as routers) can be utilised by the Control Plane to implement encrypted tunnels and tokenised or public keyed controls.

The idea here is when a client wants to talk to a service it has to prove its identity and authority to the Control Plane who then in response opens specific secure access to that client. In effect, the Control Plane implements authentication and authorisation functions directly for all the services under its control in real time. Also given all communication in effect goes over a 'public' internet, there must be blanket usage made of encrypted communications throughout.

All the Control Plane functionality can be implemented via a mature configuration management service. Often established cloud deployment frameworks come fully equipped to support this model. Which becomes extraordinarily powerful when you utilise virtualised and containerised environments as you can then spin up or down services based on their real-time trusted demand, as a service that isn't running cannot get compromised.

Now, on the face of it, this looks like a great idea, and it certainly has a lot going for it. The only downsides are the following:

1. The Control Plane is in effect a unified and Global Command and Control service; in other words, if a cybercriminal can gain control of the Control Plane then they have access to everything, or if they can interfere with the Control Plane or impersonate it, then they gain partial control or can perturb global functionality[3].

2. There is an assumption here that the network controls themselves within the services and network are without vulnerabilities, in that they provide a perfect enforcement function; they cannot, everything has a risk of compromise through its implementation.

3. There is no standard around what a Zero Trust Policy is. This often means a case by case approach to implementation with the inherent risks of functional mismatches.

4. Its implemented everywhere – so can need quite an investment up front.

5. What happens if you are using SaaS or COTS products in your business? How do they fit?

Zero Trust Networking is a useful tool in overcoming dangerous complexity when assigning trust to many systems and services, but it's not a magic bullet in ensuring security, you still need to apply the other techniques where appropriate as all security techniques have a compromise risk. It's only by combining techniques that the overall risk profile is reduced.

For instance, researchers have been able to take control of SDN (Software Defined Network) based cloud systems using the data plane (Kashyap Thimmaraju, 2018). SDN is often an implementation element of Zero Trust Networking.

---

[3] Zero Trust isn't unique in this, it is just that you are making a deliberate decision to centralise and so as a result the security of the Control Plane is critical to a successful reduction in risks.

Cryptography

We should be careful not to vilify encryption itself, which is essential for privacy, data security, and global commerce.

Mike McCaul

To keep information secure a mechanism needs to ensure only those authorised can do so. Ideally, this information protection needs to work even if stolen and loaded into another system. Encryption provides us with a means of doing so using a cryptographic key that, with an encryption algorithm, turns information into a form that is unusable without the matching decryption algorithm and key.

The process and the study of the mechanisms of using encryption and decryption technologies to protect information is known as cryptography, which has been practised and refined over hundreds of years (Singh, 1999).

Cryptography also has several other uses, particularly in:

- **Stronger authentication methods**
- **Message digests and digital signatures** – detecting unauthorised data modification
- **Non-repudiation** – enforcing association of actions or changes to a unique individual
- **Encrypted network communications** – HTTPS and secured protocols.

Given cryptography depends on complicated and time-consuming algorithms to encrypt and decrypt information, older algorithms can become subject to brute force attacks as the speed of processing available for a given cost point improves over time (in effect encryption degrades over time). Which is why the length and strength of an encryption key is an important consideration when implementing cryptography in a system, a key that is too weak or short will result in weak encryption that can be cracked in a reasonable time to make it worth trying. Also, the keys used to perform the encryption and decryption need protecting to ensure the confidentiality of the information going forward.

Cryptography algorithms fall into two broad groups: those that use a single key for encryption (symmetric-key) and decryption and those that use different keys for encryption and decryption (public-key or asymmetric key encryption). Public-key encryption has the distinct advantage that knowledge of the public key for encryption does not to give you the ability to decrypt, only the private decryption key makes that possible. In this way, the public key gets shared to all parties who need it, and if the information they send successfully decrypts using the private key (they are able to securely communicate), they can have high confidence the private key proves who the decrypting party is.

Public key cryptography can also create digital signatures, where a message is signed using the sender's private key, and the receiver can verify using the corresponding public key.

It's important to note that cryptographic algorithms are under constant refinement and enhancement in response to the efforts to find weaknesses and flaws in both their design and implementation. They can get attacked in several separate ways:

- **Brute force** – trying all combinations of keys until one matches.
- **Directed Brute Force** – based on the behaviour of an algorithm and what's discovered, the search complexity for the correct key is reduced.
- **Algorithmic Key Recovery** – a weakness in the implementation allows the development of an algorithm to analyse the usage of the cryptographic algorithm to discover the key quickly.
- **Software Bugs** – weaknesses in the implementation or its runtime environment allow its manipulation in such a way as to reveal the key.
- **Side Channel Attack** – weakness in the physical implementation of the algorithm allows the discovery of the key. For instance: direct electrical signal analysis on board, power analysis, timing, optical analysis (blinking LED's (LOUGHRY & UMPHRESS, 2002)) and electromagnetic spectrum analysis (radio transmissions).

Given the above is it essential that the use of cryptographic algorithms and their implementations get periodically reviewed, and processes are in place to update as needed in response to published vulnerabilities.

Cryptographic Back Doors

Often covered in the media is a repeated push from government agencies & politicians to have standard cryptographic algorithms with built-in back doors (a secret undocumented way to circumvent security measures) that enable law enforcement and other agencies to decrypt data easily and get hold of the information. The basis for this back-door request is with the increasing proliferation of strong encryption used to protect everything from databases & websites to chat & video sessions; it's becoming increasingly difficult for authorities to police the online world. This is also an aspect of the lag between technology and the regulations to manage its usage.

Given the current state of cryptographic algorithms such "add in" backdooring isn't possible. If a deliberate back door is put into the existing algorithms, then there will be a risk of other entities (foreign or domestic) discovering the back door and making use of it.

Also, given the freely available implementations of strong cryptography on the Internet, bad players can either choose not to use the back-doored algorithms or use the back-doored algorithms with the information inside of them already encrypted using a none back-doored algorithm (so on the outside it looks crackable but isn't). Plus, if the bad players make use of Deniable Encryption techniques, then there is no way of proving their bad intentions.

> Deniable encryption is an encryption technique where the existence of an encrypted file or message is deniable in that an adversary cannot prove the plaintext (original) exists. Essentially either multiple keys decrypt to a sensible innocent plaintext, or the encrypted text is indistinguishable in purpose from other innocent data files with it – this creates plausible deniability.

It's concerning that there is a sense of "guilty until proved innocent" occurring here, as there is a strong temptation with such a backdoor to decrypt everything flowing through the networks based on catching some bad behaviour in the act. Surveillance of communication networks do occur, but when encountering encrypted communication, this cannot be taken to indicate something bad is occurring. Instead, the parties involved might be wanting to protect their privacy and confidentiality of communication in that instance for legitimate reasons.

Also, public academics and technologists have no incentive to put backdoors into the currently strong algorithms; as they know, such backdoors will be extensively attacked until compromised to make the back door and hence the cryptographic algorithm implementing it no longer fit for purpose. It's a career dead end; nobody wants to be known for attempting to put in a back door, so no one is going to do it.

The converse of this is can also be true, the algorithms already in use may have hard to detect backdoors or flaws in them allowing discovery of the key to decrypt, and such knowledge rests with private agencies & parties who have the vast resources to enact such complex analysis. Also, state players are not beyond incentivising industry to use specific algorithms to make it easier to crack later[4]. Some academics are convinced all export strength versions of encryption algorithms have some form of backdoor (Filiol & Bannier), otherwise, why would you mandate on strength?

One could even view the public government desire to put in backdoors as a double bluff, the deed is done, and the public's tricked into thinking the encryption available is without backdoors.

For a business the only answer to this quandary is to use up to date strong encryption as part of a Defence in Depth strategy, so even if the encryption has backdoors, you still need to go through other security controls to get access to the encrypted data in the first place.

Security Process

It's often a requirement that officers of a company enact appropriate due care and diligence concerning information security. Specific steps are taken which are verifiable and measurable and that there are ongoing activities to ensure security is maintained. It must be clear that there is Security Governance enacted throughout the business.

---

[4] NSA sysadmin Edward Snowden revealed that the NSA paid RSA Security $10m to use weak Dual_EC_DBRG by default in its toolset.

Personal Information Security & Systems Architecture

Security Governance

The characteristics of security governance include:

- Enterprise-wide engagement.
- Accountable leadership.
- Seen as a business requirement.
- Defined and enforced are roles, responsibilities, and segregation of duties.
- Risks are analysed and addressed and enforced in policy & procedures.
- Sufficient resources provided.
- Staff are well trained and aware.
- Development life cycle includes security aspects.
- Planned, managed and measured.
- Regularly reviewed and audited

The effect of such governance is that security awareness and mindfulness become part of the ethos of the business.

Incident Response Plan

Security breaches do happen, despite all that is done there is a small likelihood that someone unauthorised will gain access. An incident response plan allows the reaction to such a breach to be formalised and done so to ensure it does not happen again.

An incident response plan should include the following:

- Who is in the incident response team
- Definition of the roles, responsibilities, and reporting
- Definition of a security incident
- Definition of a reportable incidents
- When training occurs
- Detection Mechanisms
- Notification Process
- Classification
- Breach Reporting Process

- Escalation Steps
- Containment Techniques and Processes
- Eradication Processes and Confirmation
- Documentation

The goal being all actors know what's needed of them and if a breach does occur it's swiftly and professionally dealt with.

Security Process Frameworks

Such processes are best defined and operated with reference to a known standard or framework. This ensures coverage and provides a consistent and proven methodology. A good starting point is the NIST Cybersecurity framework[5], which consists of standards, guidelines and best practices employed to manage security risk.

Change Management

As hinted at before, change is a dangerous thing security wise; it's a common vector by which something's missed which can critically harm security coverage and thereby leave a service or system open to attack. Change management is a formal process seeking to minimise such a risk by controlling changes to the information processing environment. Which includes anything involved in the information processing chain, be it a desktop machine or a server – all are critical to the security of the whole information flow.

Change management is especially critical with the increased use of on-demand cloud deployments and automated pushing into the production environment. It's common for what has developed anew in the morning to be in production the same day if not the following morning. In fact, quite a few businesses aim to get this release process as a short as possible, to do intraday releases.

---

[5] https://www.nist.gov/cyberframework the Framework is defined in a PDF.

From a security point of view this creates a massive headache for several reasons:

- Such a fast rate of change can often get ahead of those affected by the change, so they do not necessarily take account of it;
- Testing against other systems under such a rate of change is problematic – do they truly represent the state of play going forwards or is it going change?
- Such changes also pull in other updates as well, be they libraries or frameworks – are they secure?

Therefore, a change management process is implemented as not only a means to give security a chance to assess the change, but also to document what happened so if required they can undo the change.

Typically change management processes run as follows:

- **Initial Request**: Who wants the change, its outcome and what changed.
- **Approval**: Management reviews and signs off on the change, given the resources available and restrictions.
- **Plan**: How the change should be enacted needs planning. As well as how to back out of the change if needed.
- **Test**: Whatever's changed needs testing in a distinct environment to production yet is identical to production.
- **Schedule**: Work out when making the change is best and book it in.
- **Communicate**: Gives everyone an opportunity to comment before the change is committed just in case they missed something.
- **Implement**: At the appointed time, the change occurs, then confirmed to be successful; otherwise it's rolled back.
- **Document**: Record all the details of the change.

Such a process need not be onerous and be highly automated by the proper use of online tools and systems. Within this are embedded security controls (scanners, penetration testing, etc.), which are part of an overall automated Secure Software Development Lifecycle (SDL, SDLC or S-SDLC, pick your poison).

> Penetration testing is where a security expert attempts to break into a system as if they were a cybercriminal. This testing can either be Black Box (no awareness of the system internals), or White Box (full awareness of the internals).

Business Continuity

What's done if there is a flood at the head office, or the cloud services provider suffers a network outage?

Such situations are where Business Continuity Management (BCM) comes into effect and tries to ensure a business can continue operating in the face of such incidents. It's an integral part of a risk analysis plan as it ensures the business can keep going in case of a threat to any business function.

BCM is part architecture, part security – to do it well there needs to be an awareness of the weaknesses of technology, as well as an awareness of the risks (both internal and external) that can combine to take down systems. It stretches from understanding the mean time to failure (MTTF) of critical components and systems to the dependency interplay of systems and services. Quite often an incident failure or system behaviour change can have a dramatic unplanned knock-on effect, and it takes a keen eye to spot this and mitigate it before it occurs.

How to deal with this effectively is beyond the remit of this book, at this stage know that security is one of many critical pillars of BCM.

Security Culture

As previously hinted, it's important that the security effort be something every employee takes part in. Critical to this is the approach taken to developing a security culture or mindset within a business. Which needs an ongoing effort to educate and inform employees of their security responsibilities in a way that encourages them to interact and take on board what needs doing.

There are few simple ways to achieve this:

- Security belongs to everyone. Everyone has their part to play in making a business secure.
- Focus on awareness. Improve people's ability to see threats and combat them. Share war stories and findings.
- Put in place a secure development lifecycle and make it part of your release management process.
- Reward and recognise good security practices – celebrate the successes and encourage people to improve their training.
- Build a Community. Create a security "backbone" across the business to help people communicate and work together to solve common problems.
- Make it fun. Security isn't all about checklists and reports. Run events, use humour, turn it into a game to learn and improve.

Information Security Standards

When implementing information security, it's beneficial to the business to adopt a security standard to show compliance with a known benchmark. Also, quite a few PII regulations imply the usage of security standards to ease compliance.

The principal standard is the ISO 27001 management standard and ISO 27002 security controls standard. ISO 27001 defines an information security management system (ISMS) based on best practices. ISO 27002 details the controls used to achieve compliance, where ISO 27001 references the controls.

ISO27001 is technology and business sector agnostic and so is used by businesses of any size. It sets out precisely what the requirements are to secure information but does not specify how to go about it – leaving the business free to decide the degree of effort needed to meet their objectives and risk exposure.

A significant benefit of such a standard to a business is it can go for accredited external certification of compliance. Thus, providing proof of the protection of information assets. Such certifications are often a requirement in an increasing number of contracts going forward.

ISO 27001 Annex A lists 114 controls in 14 categories, detailed below:

- Information Security Policies
- The organisation of Information Security
- Human Resources Security
- Asset Management
- Access Control
- Cryptography
- Physical and Environmental Security
- Operations Security
- Communications Security
- System acquisition, Development, and Management
- Supplier Relationships
- Information Security Incident Management
- Information Security Aspects of BCM
- Compliance

All of these will be recognisable as aspects of information security from earlier in this chapter.

Other security standards include:

- The NIST Cybersecurity Framework (NIST CSF[6]) which provides a high-level taxonomy of cybersecurity outcomes and a methodology to assess and manage those outcomes.
- IASME[7] – a UK based standard for information assurance at small to medium-sized businesses. It enables businesses with a capitalisation of 1.2 billion pounds or less to achieve accreditation like ISO 27001 but with reduced complexity, cost and overheads.
- PCI DSS[8] – the Payment Card Industry Data Security Standard is an information security standard mandated for businesses that

---

[6] https://en.wikipedia.org/wiki/NIST_Cybersecurity_Framework
[7] https://en.wikipedia.org/wiki/IASME
[8] https://en.wikipedia.org/wiki/Payment_Card_Industry_Data_Security_Standard

handle branded credit cards from the major card schemes. Designed to reduce fraud by specific reoccurring validation of compliance against a constantly refined set of controls covering all aspects of credit card processing.

Key Points

- Information security is balancing confidentiality, integrity, and availability (CIA triad) while being efficient in policy implementation.
- Implement CIA using a Risk Management Process.
- CIA in practice maps into Communications, Hardware, and Software; then covered by Physical, Personal and Organisational aspects.
- Perform a Risk Assessment to determine assets, the risks they face and what security controls mitigate the risks.
- Security Controls are the mechanisms used to manage and minimise security threats and can be either Administrative, Logical or Physical or a combination of the three.
- Separation of Duties is the identification of roles that operate without sufficient checks and balances and splitting up the role to reduce the likelihood of abuse.
- Defence in Depth is a technique that uses multiple Security Controls that overlap to ensure security in the face of change or persistent attack.
- Information requires classification to determine its risk, and the appropriate Security Controls required.
- Access Controls control who may access and manipulate information. Access gets determined by passing the three steps of identification, authentication, and authorisation successfully.
- The Zero Trust model is a reliable way to ensure uniform service access security across many diverse services.

- Cryptography is a mechanism to protect information at rest or in transit by encryption. Businesses need to be careful to apply proven strong cryptography and keep it up to date.
- Businesses need to have transparent Security Processes and Governance that is under constant refinement and assessment.
- An Incident Response Plan codifies for a business who and how to deal with a data breach.
- Technical Change is a known risk vector for attacks and security compromises. Specific attention needs giving to designing a Change Management Process that identifies security risks before they get in production.
- Businesses Continuity Management is where the business plans its response to incidents that may affect the ongoing viability of the business.
- The Security Culture is critical to the success of information security within a business.
- ISO 27001 is an ISMS security standard whose compliance with can be externally certified.

Chapter 8
PII Anti-Patterns

If you don't know where you make your mistakes, that's
your worst mistake: not knowing where your mistakes are
at.

Meek Mill

This chapter takes a closer look at what can go wrong dealing with PII, using several common anti-patterns that make it clear what to look for and what the potential problems are.

> An anti-pattern is a common response to a recurring problem that is usually ineffective and risks being counterproductive. The term was coined in 1995 by Andrew Koenig in response to the book Design Patterns.

Anti-patterns give a handy structure for analysis and categorising the current set up. It puts the PII problems into sharp relief and provides a common language with which to discuss them.

Now described in turn is each anti-pattern, and with its features, why it's an issue and what can be done about it.

#1 Shared Role Leak

Definition: A Role exists across multiple systems with the same authentication mechanism and credentials. More than one of the systems contain PII, and this role can access it. The strict definition of the Role in of itself does not permit or sanction access to PII across multiple systems.

This anti-pattern sounds like a mistake in scoping what the Role should have access to (too broad an authorised access). Such mistakes often come about quite innocently as systems evolve or more systems get bolted onto existing access models. The temptation is just to reuse existing Roles or carbon-copy who has access to a new Role for the new system.

Its highly likely that if there are several in-house systems, that this anti-pattern is in play somewhere.

Such shared roles usually crop up in the administrative functions for a system either at an application level or a system level (SysAdmins). For instance:

- An application administrator across multiple systems could have rights to create and delete accounts, as well as modify rights, hence allow themselves to see PII.
- A database administrator can gain direct access to the database that contains and dump at will any table that could contain PII stored in the plain.
- A systems administrator is likely to have access to the backups of the databases to perform recovery operations across multiple systems.

Often such roles operate below the radar of usual logging and monitoring (or instead the way they get monitored can be manipulated). Leading to a significant PII risk that information could be dumped wholesale out of the systems concerned and nobody would be the wiser.

Take for example the case of Rigzone.com[1]. David Kent sold the site to DHI Group in 2010 for $51 million under a non-compete agreement.

---

[1]

Once the non-compete expired, he set up a similar site, oilpro.com, hoping to create another website he could sell. He managed to quickly get the membership up to 500,000 users, and DHI was interested. Then he sent out some marketing spam... He (with the help of a colleague employed at Rigzone) stole over 700,000 customer records. One of the customers of Rigzone complained he received spam from Oilpro without giving them any info. Some fake accounts were set up to test this, and they got the spam as well, proving the copying.

Note: This "god power" of admin accounts is why cybercriminals tend to target such accounts, as once in, they can quickly discover and extract information with less risk of detection.

Remediation

There are few techniques available in how to address this:

- Set up secure access logging for databases and data stores outside of the administrator's control.
- Encrypt PII at rest until used by the application.
- Move the PII into a vault service.
- Modify the application to prevent direct access to PII for administrative accounts.
- Divide upon Role access between the administrators so no one administrator can have potential access to more than one pool of PII.

Notice the ways to address falls into several main camps: more extensive monitoring and putting the PII out of reach. Each of these has pros and cons discussed later, at this stage we focus on showing the options available.

---

https://www.theregister.co.uk/2017/10/07/after_selling_site_for_millions_founder_hacked_it_for_a_second_payday/

#2 External Access Problem

Definition: A role enacted by an external third party who isn't directly under your control who has access to PII in your systems or services, or they provide systems for you on which you put your PII.

This situation typically occurs when a third party is engaged to provide a service for a system or service the business uses that contains PII, for example:

- Customer Care Outsourcing
- Offshore systems development and support

It could also be a SaaS provider who specialises in the manipulation of your PII to extract additional value (a Data Miner for instance).

There are many stories of outsourcing going wrong. A classic example happened in 2005 when Citibank had outsourced its customer support call centre to India and fraud totally $400,000 had occurred with 17 staff opening fake accounts, transferring in funds and going on luxurious holidays. Another was the $165m fraud of the ATO by a payroll processing company 'diverting' tax payments[2] for the contractors whose pay they processed.

The core problem here is that a third party who isn't part of the employee base and operating in potentially a radically different jurisdiction has access to the PII and the business is dependent upon their security to maintain the PII security. In other words, the business gets exposed to PII risks via another business, and there are no direct means to moderate those risks. This is borne out by a study (Data Risk in the Third-Party Ecosystem, 2016) that revealed 58% of respondents across multiple industries admit they cannot determine if their third-party vendor's security policies are sufficient to prevent a data breach, and only 35% say they conduct a frequent review of their chosen vendor's security measures.

---

[2] https://www.afr.com/news/policy/tax/the-inside-story-of-the-165m-scam-on-the-ato-20170519-gw8g6e

Again, this sounds like an oversight, but it can prove challenging to investigate another business to find the degree of PII risk exposure. Many businesses these days are presenting themselves as cloud-based black-box services, so there is little visibility into how they operate and where the data goes. Plus, where that data goes can change over time as a business develops. They may start out doing everything in-house and later ship it offshore to manage their costs; with no visible change to the customers (the Privacy Policy could change, but who reads them?), yet the PII risk has dramatically changed.

It may be that the offshoring operations adhere to the word of the regulations and the law accessing PII. Typically done using purely remote terminals over a secure link that have no local facility to copy and paste contents. Strictly speaking, the PII does not at any time reside in the foreign country. In such a situation two questions need answering:

- Does this set up protect the PII and how is it ensured it remains protected?
- Would the business be happy to tell their customers how they treat their PII?

If answering no to either question, stop the outsourcing as there is a risk of PII loss or severe business reputation damage.

Remediation

There are several options available:

- Require the third party to provide details of where PII is used and accessed from. Require prior notification of any change in access and processing, and the freedom to terminate without cost if the changes incur an unacceptable PII risk.
- If available, use a Service Organisation Controls (SOC) 2 report[3], which is a standard report that focusses on the IT security controls implemented by the third party.

---

[3]

https://www.aicpa.org/interestareas/frc/assuranceadvisoryservices/socguidesandpublications.html

- Require the third party to indemnify the business against any PII damage costs they may cause with the PII. Require the third party to notify you of any losses involving the PII within 24 hours.

- Require the third party to undergo a yearly security audit, the results of which get shared and are current (must have done at least one before you engage them).

- Require them to sign a PII Usage Policy, which sets out how the business expects the PII to be manipulated and conditions to meet always (later).

- Ensure they have access to the most restrictive view of the PII and still be able to perform their function (Need-to-know basis). If possible anonymise where appropriate.

If the third party does not want to share any details of their data processing architecture to assess PII security, walk away, quickly; a few reasons why:

- Given most SaaS providers implement on IaaS, as its all cloud-based, so the architecture's made up of standard components and systems – so a high-level architecture isn't proprietary or that 'magic'.

- Such unwillingness to share usually means they have something to hide, as often good architecture is something to promote and share – it's a good sign of a professional take on systems design and confidence in what's done.

- They may say that sharing such architecture information could be a security risk. The trouble with this it's a sort of admission that knowledge of the high-level architecture on its own could be sufficient to hack into their service. It strongly indicates they do not understand security is something layered on top of the architecture and that there is no such thing as security by obscurity.

Security by obscurity is the reliance on secrecy as the primary method of providing system security. Such a system could have theoretical or actual security vulnerabilities, but its owners or designers believe if the flaws are not known, that will stop a successful attack. It will not.

Regarding the indemnity of PII risks, mileage may vary on this, as it depends on how important the business is to them as a customer and their ability to entertain taking on such risks. Consider whats been paid for, especially if they give no hard guarantees or warranties for fitness of purpose of the service offered. There is also the issue that some PII regulations forbid such a free exchange of PII with third parties, in that the safeguards must be in place prior; the regulations in effect 'follow' the PII to the third party as a compliance requirement.

PII Usage Policy

A PII Usage Policy (or 3rd Party Exchange Policy) lays down strictly when PII is accessed and by whom and what its used for. It should also cover off the security of the environment in which it's accessed (office security) and if background checks and certifications are required for those accessing the PII. Do not be afraid to list what cannot occur as well, for instance:

- No cameras or other picture-taking devices (smartphones) permitted near the workstations.
- No fixed cameras or CCTV to have visibility to any screens which could contain PII.
- Take no paperwork or documentation away from workstations.
- All PII paperwork, when finished with, shred (Level-3 or better on the DIN 66399 standard[4]) or place in an approved secure document destruction facility by designated personnel.

Agreement to the PII Usage Policy must to obtained in writing before the engagement of the offshore provider. Also, if the business requires complying with ISO 27001, it's highly likely in turn that the 3rd parties will need to do so as well if they handle your PII.

---

[4] Standards on levels of document destruction via shredder. Goes from Level P-1 (lowest) to P-9 (highest, beyond military grade). Shredders that produce 'strips' are no longer secure for PII protection purposes.

Offshore Development

Offshore development faces multiple PII concerns. The most critical being how to ensure the off-shore developers are not able to access the PII storage? Most PII regulations forbid country remote 3rd parties access to PII without specific checks or barriers in place. Which can be hard to do, as often code includes configuration details that cover how the code is to access those very PII stores.

Further, even if things can be structured as to deny them access to the PII, they are writing the code which manipulates the PII, so what's to stop them putting in backdoors or flaws in the security model to enable them to gain access if required?

Then there is the problem when outsourcing the development of how to determine if the work is to the right quality to protect the PII? Required is a locally independent technical expert, with a background in security and software development, to assist with the development effort and put in the right checks and balances. This could wipe out the savings gained from off-shoring in the first place.

There are many horror stories about off-shoring development that would cause a cold sweat (data dumps appearing on the dark web; data held to ransom or deleted or just lost; backups that did not work, etc.). Unless the business can very precisely "ring fence", dependency reduce and well specify the off-shore work done, the remedial work required to bring such development up to scratch will usually wipe out all benefits including time savings. Off-shoring development is not for the inexperienced or faint of heart.

#3 Big Data Bucket Problem

Definition: Multiple systems all store their PII in one common database or data storage system. There exists (or could exist) mechanisms that permit seeing the PII across all systems easily.

This anti-pattern often crops up when a single database service or a single data storage system holds all the data for multiple systems. For instance, an HR database and Finance database that both run on the same database service. The problem is a database account is created (or already exists) that can see both the HR and Finance database from the same login.

It should be clear now why this is the Big Data Bucket Problem, as everything is sharing in the same bucket.

A variation in this is that the applications both use the same database account credentials, it just picks to which database table set it connects. So, if some cybercriminal was able to tweak the HR application to see the finance tables, we have a problem.

Such sharing often comes about as an attempt to reduce costs; it could be the HR service usage occurs out of sync with the Finance service usage, so we get decent utilisation of the shared database server. Although we suspect it's mostly a form of laziness than cost saving, as having two potentially busy databases on the one server often creates more nasty problems than it solves.

Nowadays this problem most often occurs with insecure 'secondary data dump' cloud services, such as Amazon S3 buckets. For instance, FedEx, through a subsidiary, had a publicly accessible S3 bucket containing thousands of scanned documents, including passports, driving licences and security IDs with home addresses, postal codes and phone numbers.

How to find this?

Ask the database administrators for a database deployment map that details what relevant databases per application run on which database server instances.

Which should result in a list like the one shown below:

Application	Database	Database Instance
HR	hr	db1
Finance	fin	db1
Customer Care	Cc	db2
Mailing List	Mail	db2

In the above table the HR and Finance databases both operate on the same db1 database server instance, so it could be possible to access both databases with the same credentials.

It also looks like the Customer Care, and Mailing List databases are on the same db2 database server instance; so, in this example, we have two "database buckets" that both contain PII from different systems, so there is a possibility of cross talk here as well.

Remediation

The sharing needs breaking, and is done as follows:

- Put the PII into two distinct database services or data stores that do not share the same access credentials.
- Alternatively, move the PII into a dedicated vault fit for the purpose (more later)
- Alternatively, encrypt the PII at rest using a distinct encryption or keying scheme per database or data store. The downside with this is your queries will not be able to make use of the PII fields directly, a surrogate field will need implementing that is sufficient (later).

It might be that we achieve the same separation using a middleware layer that in effect does the routing to the right database on behalf of the applications. The trouble is this enforces the separation remotely, in that if someone was to get access to the credentials and gain access to the database, they would still be able to see everything (or pretend to be the other app by hacking the middleware). So the middleware is a fudge and does not adequately address the core risk.

There might be complaints about potentially increased costs, although usually, these will not eventuate at the level implied as one giant database instance is split into several smaller ones, which tends to offset the expected running costs. Also, the individual databases can scale appropriately to match their loading, again reducing the running costs. Spinning up new database instances in the cloud is very much an automated undertaking and having multiple instances isn't onerous if serious.

The golden rule is if it should be apart, it needs to be physically apart.

Also, as mentioned above, check where all the scanned files, attachments or PDF's get stored for the databases and make sure its private.

#4 Zombie PII

Definition: Keeping PII in a system or service on the basis that it might prove useful in the future. Where on examination the information is either out of date or not fit for purpose.

On the face of it keeping hold of PII sounds like an excellent idea for a business, given it's mined to discover facts and improve existing products and services. Although the value of PII, like all information, degrades over time; for several reasons:

- People move, get married, divorced and eventually die.
- People change their tastes, preferences, and their likes and dislikes over time.
- People physically change over time.
- The social and economic situations of people change over time.

It's usually best to regard the PII as a "snapshot" of a person's state at a given moment in time (assuming everything about them is in sync with how up to date it is). Beyond the time of the snapshot, it will progressively become less accurate. Also, the business itself might change its focus, so the business value of the PII on file will change in response to that (it can be no longer be applied in the way intended).

So over time PII not cleaned out regularly will turn into zombie data (it's certainly no longer information). Which can be quite dangerous for several reasons:

- If used in business decision making, the wrong decisions might be made.
- Storage of archived data does not have the best security qualities (tapes do go missing).

Plus, there is the cost of keeping all this zombie PII shuffling around the storage systems on the off chance it could be useful. There is also the significant risk that PII regulations could painfully bite concerning holding onto no longer required PII.

Remediation

Given PII has a known shelf life, the solution is to add support to the systems to track its shelf life in detail. Which is done as follows:

- Per record of PII add in fields to track the last modification data of the most valuable PII fields (does not have to be all the fields). Update this whenever the associated PII field changes (even if it's the same content).

- Define a PII Retention Policy to state exactly how long to keep different PII in the systems if not updated and the methods by which PII is validated. Usually a blanket time with a few specific exceptions.

- Codify into the systems identification of PII that is about to expire – mark as about to expire and enact the automated validation process.

- Codify into the systems identification of PII that has expired – delete it.

Also, if there is no valid use for the PII in question, delete it wholesale and stop collecting it – the safest PII is that not held.

PII Validation

Validation of the correctness of PII occurs in two ways:

- During an engagement with the person whose PII it is, this is usually via customer care or if the customer enacts with a product in an identifiable way;

- Via a communication to the person in question, either via post or email.

Do be careful to do this in a way that prevents identity theft (see later).

#5 Fractured PII

Definition: Copies of the same PII get kept in different systems for convenience or historical design reasons. When the PII is updated on one system that change isn't made to the other system, resulting in differences in the PII between the systems.

Systems love to hold onto information and PII is no exception to this rule. The trouble is that lots of systems and processes within a business depend on PII, so the tendency is to copy and record PII into whatever system needs it. Which creates many problems:

- There is no guarantee of PII consistency in the systems, it's free to duplicate, fracture and become distinct.
- Given PII is a security risk, this means all the systems that store PII needs suitable security, which can be expensive.
- The fact data is copied can often bloat the storage requirements and prevent optimisations in the flow of data through a business.
- It can also cause duplicate phantom records, where there are two or more distinct customers but only really one.
- It encourages conditions that breed Zombie PII.

Also given the mandatory disclosure of PII requirements in most regulations, each system needs visiting to construct the PII Report for an inquiry – which can be painful to organise and ensure is secure.

How to find this?

First, find where the same PII is stored in a given workflow, it should be straightforward to see how the PII progresses with the diagrams developed. Then ask the system owners what they do when PII updates and if they pass on the update to the source system. If the answer is no, there is a point of fracture. Another way this can occur is if the source system does update it's PII, but the receiving system won't update its copy.

Fracturing discovery might be based on feedback from customers and third parties who are frustrated at the inconsistencies.

Remediation

The solution to this is simple if challenging to implement: for each pool of PII (distinct and no overlapping usage case), there is a single dedicated system that keeps the PII on behalf of all the others. No other system can keep a persistent local copy of PII; it must always refer to the 'Source of Truth' for the latest and greatest PII. Having a temporary copy is fine if removed once used.

> A Source of Truth is a system that is the keeper of a specific class of information to which other systems refer.

Note the use of "dedicated system", this is important. Such a function cannot just bolt onto an existing system, as it's likely that system will not have the right operational and security characteristics for such a critical function (a bit like putting a rocket on a car, it could go off in the wrong direction at any time). For instance, do not bolt this onto an order processing framework or a customer facing website backend. Given how cheap it's now to spin up dedicated system instances at whatever scale point needed, there is no excuse for not doing this correctly.

Details on this are described later.

#6 Chop Suey PII

Definition: PII, when stored in a system, gets truncated or shortened in a way which makes the PII incorrect and not possible to process successfully.

Not such a problem these days but it still does crop up from time to time. Truncation of PII most often will show up in names, telephone numbers and addresses as these vary the most between countries and locales. At some point, such information gets recorded or communicated via a fixed field structure, and there is a risk of it truncating or causing a programming bug or potentially a security bug.

The security problem occurs when too long a string is written into a fixed program structure and causes the string to overwrite what's after it in memory, either causing the program to crash or "execute" the long string as is (which can give a cybercriminal control), known as stack buffer overflow.

How to find this?

Determine what name, address and telephone numbers are fixed fields in the systems and then get the maintainers of such systems to look for these fields when they match exactly the length they should be stored in – chances are this is where something truncates. Examine and find out if this is the case.

It might be that end users, and customers have complained about this problem in the past as well.

Remediation

First, the PII fields that are truncating need increasing in length based on measured lengths of the fields in other systems or on agreed standard lengths for such fields.

Then see if the truncated information is recoverable from other systems or go back to the original persons affected to correct the information as stored, assuming there is sufficient correct information to be able to do so. Otherwise, the incorrect record is deleted, as it's not fit for purpose.

#7 Lost in Translation

Definition: *PII when transferred between systems, storage or language framework undergoes a transformation that introduces errors.*

Most people have encountered this at some time or other, in its purest form dashes, commas, hyphenations and significant spaces can go missing; the texts are still readable, just not the same. For instance, the surname De Souza becomes Desouza, or the double-barrelled surname Hilbert-Smith becomes Hilbertsmith, or O'Donnell becomes ODonnell[5]. In its worst form, the whole text becomes unreadable as something that looks like random characters typed by a particularly jetlagged drunken typist – otherwise known as Mojibake.

> Mojibake (文字化け) – is Japanese for "character transformation" and refers to the garbled text that is the result of text being decoded using an unintended character encoding.

How to find this?

The simplified form is found with reference to the original unmodified text, by searching for records in other systems that are missing characters. Alternatively, a character usage analysis per system is done for the same types of PII types, those systems which restrict certain characters should have 'blanks' in their distribution.

There are several ways to detect Mojibake:

- Exact field to field comparison being sensitive to the character sets in use.
- Comparing text lengths either one by one or by using a distribution analysis.
- Comparing by eye. Usually, the users will notice it by this route first.

---

[5]   https://www.kalzumeus.com/2010/06/17/falsehoods-programmers-believe-about-names/

> A character set consists of characters encoded in a certain way in a computer system. When moving characters to another character set, you need to carefully map or recode to avoid minimising loss (where a character does not exist in the target character set). The overly simplistic mapping between character sets is a cause of one form of Mojibake.

Also look out for issues where everything appears fine in your systems, yet when using the information in another context, it suddenly becomes garbled – say on a website or in an email. Proving the display context either has an incorrect representation of the text (wrong actual encoding) or the context does not make the right choice on how to display it (wrong character set assumed).

Remediation

Before fixing this problem, its source needs to be determined; namely is it an underlying filtering/stripping action or a character set encoding problem.

For the filtering/stripping action, find out why it's there and if it's needed; usually it isn't. Remove it and make sure where the information gets stored can cope with the new characters. Once confirmed, reimport the affected fields.

For fixing Mojibake, make sure the impacted system is using a large enough character set – nowadays there is little excuse for not using Unicode everywhere.

> Unicode is a computing industry standard for the consistent encoding, representation, and handling of text expressed in most of the world's writing systems, Currently up to version 10.

Check if the underlying storage system can cope with the change to Unicode and that the programs which use it can cope with Unicode. Then hire a security and internationalisation professional who is familiar with fixing Mojibake issues – there are many edge cases that need dealing with. There must be 100% confidence that Unicode will work everywhere as intended and doesn't create a security problem somewhere else. This problem is because Unicode has of well over 100,000 characters; quite a few are visually remarkably similar and often transform to smaller character sets as the same character. Thereby allowing security injections to bypass filters and successfully attack a target. Such similarities can also trick users.

It should also be remembered; it's usually impossible to recover from the garbled text the original text – the original text is needed. If it's not available, either contact the original persons impacted or delete the records, they are not fit for purpose.

#8 PII Paper Trail

Definition: PII entered by hand into computer systems off paper-based forms or notes, and there is no mechanism to destroy the paper records securely.

If a business answers the phone or processes post, at some point, recorded on a piece of paper is PII, either as something sent in or created in-house. This action on its own isn't wrong, as often someone might not be at the computer to enter the information. The trouble comes when that piece of paper is finished with and where it ends up. If it's just put in a bin or left on a desk that isn't the proper way to deal with the PII.

Also, if such paperwork is filled away, what happens when it's no longer needed? Which means the way the paper gets stored must be secure and tracked.

How to find this?

Finding unsecured paper-based PII is often as easy as just checking people's desks and what's in the bins. Also check around photocopiers, printers and fax machines. Then have a look at what's the filing cabinets and if they are locked with the keys kept secure.

Remediation

The solution to this depends on whether the step of the information going on paper in the first place can go. In an ideal world, the computer application for PII entry is always available, thereby removing the need to record anything on paper.

If the paper recording step is unavoidable, then provide a secure means of destroying the paper after its used. Usually by some form of shredder (actively destroy the document after use, or place into a secure document destruction bin, this is a locked bin where the contents are taken periodically and destroyed). Also, there should be a 'clean desk' policy put in place for people handling paper-based PII.

If documents are for long-term storage, receiving legal documents that people have put their PII onto for example, then store the documents in a suitably secured cabinet that's always locked. Do investigate digital scanning and storage as an alternative, or digital document signing and cut out the whole paper process. The less paperwork a business needs to keep the better the security.

Chapter 9
PII Strategies

Sound strategy starts with having the right goal

Peter Drucker

This chapter describes some specific security strategies or techniques that apply to systems and information to make PII more secure. Also looked at is some more significant business operational strategies. This can be considered part of an overall Privacy by Design[1] (PbD) technical strategy that implements the 7 Foundational Principles[2].

Is PII Really Needed

Before considering the technical strategies regarding manipulating PII, establish first if there is a solid business case for having PII. There are two main reasons for this:

- Most PII regulations require a valid business case and so a reason for having PII in the first place.
- The less PII a business is responsible for, the less risk of a serious breach.

The first reason is unavoidable, the regulations often require documented reasons to process PII and need agreeing prior with the individuals impacted. The second is a strategic question, with handling PII there are associated risks and costs, so there needs to be an evident return.

---

[1] https://en.wikipedia.org/wiki/Privacy_by_design
[2] https://www.ipc.on.ca/wp-content/uploads/Resources/7foundationalprinciples.pdf

145

Consider if PII needs to be handled 'as is' or if it can be anonymised. If anonymised successfully (it cannot be reversed) it puts the information outside of the scope of PII regulations, as it can never refer to an individual.

If there is PII that needs keeping as is, the business will need to:

- Provide appropriately secure storage of such information;
- Catalogue PII processing;
- Implement a PII expiry policy;
- Seek opt-in agreement from all the individuals to the processing;
- Record access to, distribution of and usage of the PII.
- Author a privacy policy that details PII usage.

They will also need to provide processes for the individuals to access, modify, export or delete their PII. As well as processes to respond to regulatory enquiries and appropriate management oversight of the compliance effort.

As explained, the less PII processed and stored, the fewer resources required to fulfil PII regulatory requirements and the less the risk of breach. Remember business value from PII comes from what's done with it, not the act of keeping it.

PII Straight to Store

Something that needs sorting out early on is the quicker PII gets into the secured system and stored the better for all. In other words, try to streamline processes to avoid manual or paper-based steps to getting the PII into the system. The goal here is for all significant workflows in the business that involve PII *nothings* stored anywhere else, even temporarily.

So, for instance:

- Sales answering the phone and making paper notes – instead, provide a proper online sales lead management solution.

- Forms come in via post, fax or email that need entering and storage – look at either scanning to digital storage or direct digital signing of online forms.

Be quite determined on this, the more streamlined the processes to remove the need for the physical manipulation of PII this will both reduce the security risks and reduce the business costs at the same time. The trick is to look at the information entered and see if the party who originally wrote down the information can type that instead directly into a computer system the business operates.

This streamlining also avoids people being 'caught' between systems, in that they are a manual physical step between what could be two computer systems that could directly be talking to each other.

Defence in Depth Redux

Explained in *Core Information Security Principals* is Defence in Depth as a strategy to secure systems, the fundamental idea is to have a layered approach to securing systems to make it that much harder for a cybercriminal to gain access and successfully steal information.

On the face of it, this sounds like a robust approach to take, but there are few real-world aspects of how systems are set it up which need to be correct for it to be effective.

First off, most approaches to Defence in Depth concentrate on the classic Onion diagram as shown below.

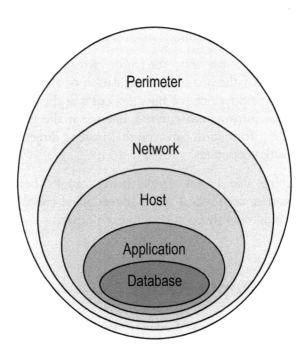

Figure 8 - Classic Onion Diagram

The trouble with this diagram is it's a 2-dimensional view of a complex interplay between a whole variety of systems and services, both physical and logical. At each level, it implies an actor or agent can only move up or down when they can often move laterally or 'jump' a layer depending on where they are, whom they are pretending to be and what they are doing.

Also, the controls put at one layer which might prevent them doing something dangerous in more inner layers can get sidestepped by 'smuggling' that dangerous action through the control.

In real life, the interplay between the layers and a set of systems in a typical business is more like multidimensional snakes and ladders board crossbred with a labyrinth on a bad hair day, and cybercriminals know this and use it to their advantage. For instance, everything computer based in a business can be accessed both logically (via the services it provides) and physically (inserting a CD or USB thumb stick or just turning off). Plus, the people who look after the computers (logically and physically) can be accessed as well (plus the cleaners, maintenance people, etc.). So, there are at least two other dimensions of interaction not shown by the Onion diagram.

Also, remember such an Onion diagram is just looking at a single system and the protection implemented around it, nothings said about what protection (if any) exists around other systems that might have access to (just in case backdoors) or knowledge of (shared passwords anyone?) the system in question. So, there is another hidden dimension of the system to system interaction and information leakage to take into consideration as well.

What's also not shown is how discoverable each layer is and what it does in response to an attack. Does it just sit there like a lemon and let an attacker continue trying until they succeed? Will it react and what occurs? Does a layer ease "setting up base camp" so the cybercriminal can come back quickly to it later (leaving something to watch what's going on)?

Remember a cybercriminal does not need to break in all in one go. If able they will happily progressively work their way inwards until they get what they want. They know security gets often implemented in a 'naive' way with often little understanding of how cybercriminals operate. Cybercriminals also know the sheer complexity of modern computing systems provide a massive playground for them to operate in. It's not unheard of for IT staff to discover a compromise some months after the initial attack, or the first sign of a compromise is when the cybercriminals want a ransom paid.

Zero Trust Model

One of the possible ways to deal with this mess is to adopt the Zero Trust Model and centralise Authentication and Authorisation models within a Control Plane that enforces fine-grain access control with always encrypted transports. See Chapter 7 for a more detailed description of Zero Trust Networking.

This model will help a lot but do not depend 100% on any one security technique or solution to provide a complete solution – instead combine different techniques as needed to ensure appropriate management of security risks.

Get to know your Cybercriminal

To defend a system against a cybercriminal requires knowing how they operate. Fundamentally cybercriminals proceed based on information they can gather about a system they are hacking. Further, the amount of effort a hacker will undertake is related to the value of what they *think* they will find and the risks of capture or profiling. Where the risk of capture relates to the amount of time needed to hack a system (the longer it takes, the more likely enough information's collected about the hacker to profile[3] or catch them, assuming robust logging services).

Also, like everyone, cybercriminals have bills to pay and mouths to feed, so they need an expected rate of return for effort undertaken. Or look at this another way, they cannot afford to spend too long or too much on breaking into a system for which there isn't enough clear return or reward. Plus, there are always plenty of more fish in the sea, namely other easier to hack systems with higher returns, they only need find them.

The following equation neatly represents this interplay:

$$reward = v * \frac{s + c - p}{r}$$

Equation 1 - Cybercriminals Reward Equation

---

[3] Profiling is collecting and analysing information on the hacker's activity to lead to discovery and capture.

Where:

> *reward* = what a cybercriminal gets from a hack
> s = system information that visible[4] (0 to 1)
> v = protected information value to the cybercriminal
> p = probability of capture (0 to 1)
> c = system compliance to the cybercriminal (0 to 1)
> r = resources the cybercriminal has available.

Remember this is looking at this from the cybercriminal's perspective, the more positive the reward value, the more likely a cybercriminal will succeed in getting something of value to them out of a system. Whereas a negative value indicates its unlikely the cybercriminal will get something of value without capture.

So, to a cybercriminal an ideal system to hack is one that:

- Contains (or gives access to, hence why authentication services are targeted first) lots of valuable information (PII and SPII in particular),
- Has a low probability of being caught,
- Takes little effort to hack, and,
- The system is predictable and informative.

Note#1: Whatever units this equation is in doesn't matter, it's the relative interplay of the values we are looking at.

Note#2: The probability of capture could either be the probability as seen by the hacker or our probability of catching them, the two need not be the same, used to beneficial effect later.

So, in the Defence in Depth model, what can be done, knowing this equation, to put off the cybercriminal?

First off, let's limit the cybercriminal's ability to get an accurate knowledge of the systems, causing them to spend more resources working out how to hack the systems, which improves the odds of catching or stopping them. In effect, s goes down, whilst p goes up, and r must increase to compensate

---

[4] All systems on a network have a visible 'footprint' used to figure out what a system is and hence what exploits to try against it.

for the lack of information, result being a decreased reward for the cybercriminal. More later how to do this and play with their minds a bit.

Secondly, also reduce the degree of compliance shown to the cybercriminal by the systems at each layer. This means the system both recognises an attack and responds in kind to frustrate the attack by usually locking them out for a time.

The trouble is, cybercriminals know this and have several strategies to deal with timeouts and lockouts, usually involving a whole fleet of cheap zombie machines[5] to try and brute force their way into a system (or at least reveal more information about a system to fine-tune the attack). So, slightly reduced compliance isn't the roadblock it once was as cybercriminals can play for time now across multiple target systems at once with ease.

Automated Hacking

The Hollywood image of a cybercriminal is someone pouring over lines of green on black code on a monitor in a dark room to find the magic combination to get in. While some do operate this way, the majority use scripts and toolkits. Attack automation is to such a level that the cybercriminal only gets involved when the automation informs them of a successful attack. Also, such scripts tend to run on zombie machines they took over or 'rented' from a dark web provider for the task.

Now this automation has made the cybercriminal's job easier, but it also makes the attacks very formulaic and subject to manipulation to our advantage.

---

[5] Otherwise known as bot nets, groups of machines hijacked by hackers under centralised command and control to do their bidding.

It's Okay to Lie to Cybercriminals

Typically, such scripted dictionary attacks depend upon the attacked system being 100% honest, namely when finding a username and password to match the system reports that they have indeed found a valid set of login credentials.

Let's mess with the cybercriminals mind a bit and do the following:

1. Recognise when a system is under attack.
2. When the attacker matches some credentials or information set, report it as a failure.
3. When an attacker fails to match, at a given probability, report it as a success.

A cybercriminal faced with such a system will not know they're recognised as an attacker and assume the information returned is correct when it's not. In this way, the cybercriminal has false information that *only they* can have, so that information could allow discovery of the cybercriminal (if they are silly enough to use it directly themselves, it has been known). The key is the probability of injecting a false-positive needs to be low enough for the hacker to not notice the difference, but high enough for them to not spend an inordinate age on it – on the basis that even cybercriminals can get "lucky" sometimes[6].

What's refreshing about this approach is the manipulation of the cybercriminal's signal to noise ratio concerning a system without them being aware of it. It's rare security professionals can get to turn the tables on the cybercriminals in such a comprehensive and sneaky way.

Going back to the cybercriminal's reward equation, by such comprehensive barefaced lying to the cybercriminal the effective compliance value has been set to zero (they don't know this has occurred from their side) – so unknown to the cybercriminal their reward value has gone to zero as well as they are not going to get in.

It's also important to note that such a technique will work with any system a cybercriminal is trying to manipulate to their advantage. It's not limited

---

[6] If you intend to go down this route, contact the author, there are some subtle tricks to make this fully effective.

to username and password dictionary attacks, *any* attack that depends on progressive information discovery can be severely perturbed if not totally 'bent' using this technique. Also, if implemented properly, the cybercriminal will have no way of knowing when faced with several equivalent systems which are the ones that could be lying. This creates a 'herd immunity' effect.

Also, the knowledge of them being a cybercriminal can carry into the system as they go (using back-channel analysis looped to the SIEM or in session or user record flags), so such compliance manipulation could occur anywhere in the Defence in Depth model and follow them around.

This technique is a form of Runtime Application Self-Protection[7] (RASP) built right into the application, where the application responds to the attack to prevent it from being successful, whilst potentially aiding the discovery of the cybercriminal, which is the real sting in the tail for the cybercriminal.

If you do implement such a RASP technique, it's important that its ties into the Efficient Security Response (ESR) Methodology, so it's known when the response triggers to watch out for usage of the poisoned payload.

It's important to note that this technique won't provide protection if the hacker is able to get underneath the application and access operating level services, the assumption is there is sufficient integrity in the application framework to prevent that. Although similar watch, mark, and respond techniques can apply here too.

Camouflaging

Likewise, systems can also lie about what they declare themselves to be. A systematic camouflage that fools the cybercriminal into thinking the systems are one form of system when they are something completely different. So, the amount of system information visible is the same, it's just not correct (compliance goes down again). This way they spend time trying to attack a system that isn't there. This is also an odd form of implied honeypot.

---

[7] https://en.wikipedia.org/wiki/Runtime_application_self-protection

> A honeypot is a security mechanism set to detect, deflect, or, in some manner, counteract attempts at unauthorized use of information systems.

Such camouflaging is best on systems that face directly onto the public internet, such as websites.

A website administrator can choose to leave on the default configurations, which will often per request broadcast:

- What the web server software is and its version,
- The programming language used,
- If there are any optional modules turned on,
- Even the software framework used.

To us, this is the website equivalent of having a satellite image map detailing what alarm system a house uses and which are unlocked doors.

Armed with such detailed information a cybercriminal has two choices:

- Use it now to work out what attacks work against the website, or,
- Keep a note of the information, so when a good exploit becomes available, come back to the website and try it.

If instead, the defaults are off or in their place are 'fake' values, the cybercriminal either finds out nothing about the system or gets duff information. Either way, the systems have become harder to crack as they have less information to use.

Now some may think this is a form of security by obscurity – it's not, something isn't unprotected for a cybercriminal to just locate. Instead, the signal to noise ratio they get from sniffing is modified to our advantage.

Strong Suggestion to System and Framework Authors:

Please:

1. Make it extremely easy to turn off or modify all such inline announcements, do not require additional modules or plugins to do so, this should be standard;
2. By default, have them *all* turned off.

Knock Knock, Who's There?

One cannot discuss camouflage without mentioning port-knocking[8]. This is a technique where a service is kept hidden (via firewall rules) from the general Internet until a specific series of connections are seen against a set of predefined ports, then the rules are changed to make the hidden service visible to the IP of the 'knocking' remote machine. In this way automated crawlers or attackers who don't know how to knock won't see the hidden service, saving a lot of resources that otherwise would have to deal with all the cybercriminal sniffing traffic. It's important to note that the protected service still needs securing independently of the port knocking protection.

Cybercriminals often use port-knocking themselves as a way of hiding a backdoor into a compromised system, it won't show up on normal network scans.

Defence in Depth Qualities

So, given all the above, what are the qualities to look for in a Defence in Depth implementation? Look for at least the following:

- **Strong Separation** – each layer should operate distinctly from other layers where ever possible. This stops a chain reaction if a layer's breached and removed.

---

[8] https://en.wikipedia.org/wiki/Port_knocking

- **Independence** – each layer performs its own access checks and balances without trust depending upon any other layer.
- **Fail Safe** – if a layer goes down, it doesn't just disappear and permit access.
- **Verified** – correct operation of a layer in securing a system needs proving.
- **Monitored** – if a layer does get compromised there needs to be an independent way of being notified, so a cybercriminal cannot just 'cut the wires' and keep going without an alert going out.

Given all the above that needs doing to keep PII secure, this leads to the next strategy.

Funnels

Most implementations of Defence in Depth forget to set up the layers so that an inner layer will only respond or interact 'outwards' with the next outward calling layer. The idea is the outer layer if compromised or bypassed; then the inner layer will ignore the foreign requests. See the next diagram for an example of how this works.

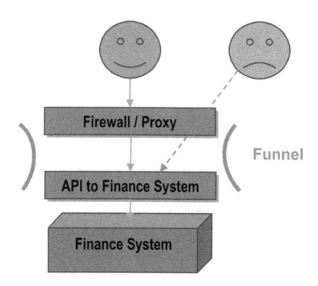

Figure 9 Defence in Depth Funnelling

In the above diagram, the smiley-faced user can access through the firewall (which might do its own auth or have client restrictions), and hence via the proxy on the back of the firewall access the finance system API, as the proxy has been 'blessed' on a whitelist to have access to the finance system. Whereas the sad-faced cybercriminal, even if they 'jump' the firewall, unless they can get to the proxy, the finance system API will not process their requests, hence the dashed line, it won't work unless they come in via a system on the whitelist.

The trick is not to overly trust the outer layers by locking down what's accepted from the outer layers. In this way, you create a 'funnel' around the defence in depth layering which forces a hacker to engage only via those layers in the order implemented. Such whitelisting can use:

- A restricted list of client IP's.
- A token added in by the proxy which could even be a signing token for the requests.

An additional refinement is to also operate the funnel principal the other way around, in that the inner layer may only talk to its immediate upper layer. This makes more difficult to exfiltrate data (copying data to a system outside of business control) from a compromised system and stops generic command and control communications. This could cause an impact on legitimate external traffic (such as updating and patching activity) – although specific whitelisting / proxy or offline updating and snapshotting can make this workable.

All PII Access is Logged

In the case of either a data breach or to fulfil an individual's right of access, there is a need to make sure to log all access to PII and that the logs archive is a secure manner.

Now on the face of it, this sounds like a daunting task that's going to result in lots of logs clogging up systems at great expense, but it need not have to be that way, for several reasons:

- Accessing PII either by an individual as a manual action or a system as part of some automated process.
- Accessing PII either as an individual record or as part of a whole batch of records.

Such accesses can classify into two types:

- **PII preserving requests** – the PII is delivered or seen as is.
- **PII hiding requests** – the PII is anonymised so as not to refer to an individual.

So, the PII hiding requests don't need logging, as the PII isn't visible or seen, which is the whole point. This defines a matrix of outcomes as follows:

		Who or What's accessing	
		Individual Person	System
What is accessed	**Single Record**	Logged	Access Recorded
	Batch of Records	Logged as Batch	Access Recorded

The detailed logging occurs around when an individual does something, so either log in detail what specific record's accessed, when they do so and what they did, or record what 'set' of records were accessed. The batch operation could very well be a dump or a selection of records, recording the parameters used to select that is fine.

The access recorded option is just to note somewhere that a remote system made request for either a single or batch of records, the goal here being to record the dependency and hence route the PII went, as the other system, in turn, will record activity based on the matrix shown above, leaving in effect a breadcrumb trail.

Remember, there are two reasons for logging, the first is to fulfil the individual's right of access to know what's being stored on them and how that's used. The second is to deal with a data breach and work out exactly what the cybercriminals (or insiders) had access to and what they did.

To show this working in practice, see the next diagram.

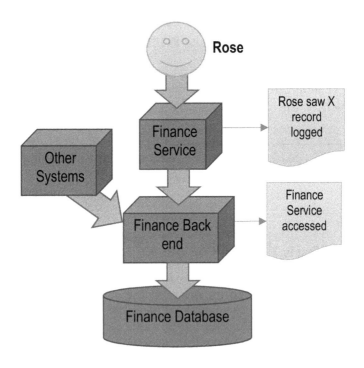

Figure 10 - Logging PII Access

Rose, the friendly rosy faced account manager, needs to see PII information relating to customer X. They log into the Finance Service and navigate to the screen where they can enact accessing the PII of X. When they enact the request, write two log records:

- The fact that Rose saw the PII of X, and,
- The fact the Finance Service accessed the Finance Back End.

Is this way it's recorded both who accessed the PII and what system was using the Back End to access the PII, thereby completing a chain of logging.

Where to log

Just as important as the act of logging is keeping such logs secure, in that, once written, they cannot be altered or deleted, or at least tampering with the logs can be detected after the fact. It's not enough to record the logs alongside the records they relate to in the same database, for what should be obvious by now reasons.

Depending on how sensitive the PII is, it might be worth looking at technologies like Blockchain or chained record signing[9] to ensure logs, as recorded, cannot change without detection. Also, consider combining this with a timestamping service[10] to provide an independent signature that cannot be forged from the control of the logging service alone. Also, strongly consider if the logs need to be part of a BCM plan, given their criticality to ensuring integrity.

It's also important that the logs are indexed and hence searchable when required. No point having mountains of logs that take days to trawl through, search requests must be responded to quickly. Luckily there are open source and cloud-based services[11] which provide suitable logging services. Just make sure the logs don't leak PII of their own, they should only contain actions and references to what occurred.

---

[9] Hash-based message authentication code (HMAC) or equivalent cryptographic signatures that utilise chaining, so log record deletion as well as modification is detectable. In effect the previous record hash value combines with the current record (plus secret) to create the new hash value.

[10] On periodic basis a generated hash is sent to a standalone service which utilises public/private keying to generate a timestamped signature to then store back in the log. https://en.wikipedia.org/wiki/Trusted_timestamping

[11] Papertrail, Logz.io, Logsene are examples of suitable log management software.

PII Man In The Middle

When PII travels over a network or equivalently visible transport, there must be confidence that:

- The transmitted PII was received without error or modification.
- Anybody else seeing the communication cannot extract the PII for themselves[12]

Confidence is obtained by using a suitable encryption method on top of an error correcting transport (TLS over TCP/IP for instance). It's essential to understand that this is no absolute, as the strength of the encryption used decides how secure the information is from eavesdroppers.

Where is this Needed?

There are several key places in a system where care needs taking to protect PII communications, these usually are:

- The end customer (either via browser or app) accessing the applications or services that contain PII;
- Employees accessing PII containing services from desktop machines, laptops, tablets and smartphones.
- Usage of cloud-based services that manipulate PII.

This isn't an exhaustive list, but the fundamental principle is if PII ever goes over a network which isn't 100% trusted is secure for PII, the PII in transit needs encrypting. This can extend to communications with database servers in a colocation facility, one lousy configuration update, and the traffic might be open to the world. In fact, adopt the Zero Trust mindset and *always* encrypt PII in transit, this could be simpler to implement as it's consistent.

---

[12] This is a Man in the Middle (MITM) attack as something in the network is harvesting the communications unknown to both parties.

Examples of the types of acceptable protocols and standards to use are as follows:

- Websites / REST– HTTPS TLS 1.2 with weak cryptographic algorithms turned off (MD5 and SHA-224) or use TLS 1.3[13].
- Databases – client to server connections with TLS 1.1 or better with weak algorithms turned off.

The fundamental principle is to turn on encryption by default and do not allow unencrypted or weakly encrypted transports to connect. Ideally, use TLS 1.3 if possible.

PII at Rest

PII is stored somewhere within systems, either in a database, a file storage mechanism or a temporary file if being relocated. The question is how to handle that information to be secure and follow the regulations always?

The trouble with PII at rest is that if stored in the plain (no encryption) then its safety is dependent upon the layers of protection around it and what controls limit access. If those controls should fail, or are incorrectly implemented, then it's easy for a hacker or thief[14] to copy the PII right out.

Here are several real-world examples that prove the point:

- A misconfigured Amazon S3 bucket compromised 48,270 PII records of Australian employees working in government agencies, banks, and a utility company. The PII included full names, passwords, IDs, phone numbers, email addresses and some credit card numbers, along with some salary and expense details. (Nov 2017)
- PII for 9,400 job seekers accessed via an insecure Amazon S3 bucket. (Sept 2017)

---

[13] Just approved March 2018 so will become widely available within a year.
[14] Laptop stolen from the software developer's car containing the names, Social Security numbers and credit card details for 84,000 University of North Dakota alumni. (Oct 2008)

- Via an insecure Amazon S3 bucket, 2.2 million customer records for Dow Jones & Company exposed. (May 2017)
- The PII of 550,000 blood donors exposed on the Red Cross website by a contractor. The PII included names, gender, addresses and dates of birth. (Oct 2016)

So those 4 examples alone resulted in the exposure of over 2.8 million records of PII. It's clear from the rate of breaches occurring and their size that this is a security problem that needs specific attention to solve.

And the solution is…

Given the volume of PII involved and damage that results from a leak, it's necessary that a 'belt & braces' approach is taken, namely:

- PII, when stored in bulk (such as a flat file, archive or dump of records), **must** be encrypted and require a specific key to decrypt[15].
    o Copying PII in the plain to a storage device then encrypting it is expressly **forbidden**[16].
- PII, when stored individually on a shared service (a drive, file store, or key-value store shared between multiple applications.), **must** be encrypted and require a specific key on access to decrypt.
- Never store the key with the PII.
- Periodically test the access controls around the storage system to ensure they deny unauthorised access.

The idea here is even if the access controls fail, anyone looking at the files cannot do anything with them without the key. So even if a dump of PII gets into the public domain, the risk of the decrypting the dump in a viable timeframe is too low to be of concern. The encryption needs to be strong enough to be virtually unbreakable for at least 25 years, after that time most of the information will be out of date.

---

[15] Hardware level encryption is not enough, as this is often automatic, the accessing application must have to apply the key to decrypt.
[16] Copies of the plain PII can still exist on the storage or the copying itself occurred over a transport medium not encrypted, see PII Deletion later for an explanation.

Key generation and management

For such an approach to remain secure, it's vital that sufficient key length[17] is used, so the PII remains secure for the foreseeable future. It's also important that key storage is very secure; they are the keys to the kingdom. A service which encrypts the keys at rest with strong access controls and multisite storage would be ideal.

Depending on the value of the PII in the system consider using multiple keys in a key table indexed off some identifier per record, for example:

- Generate a table of 100 keys (3072-bit length)
- Derive a hash function which given a PII record ID turns that into an index into the key table.
- Use that key to encrypt the PII data in that given record.

In effect create 100 different "encryption spaces" within the one PII table. So even with knowledge of the hash function, it forces a hacker to deal with 100 keys to break instead of one, increasingly the resources needed 100-fold[18], which according to the hacker reward equation reduces the reward a 100-fold as well. This would act as a particularly good deterrent, as it shows the encryption used isn't as straightforward as it appears.

Alternatively, remove the hash function and put in a key index field with the PII in the record[19], ideally using space expansion[20] to make it look like more keys are in play. As again the knowledge of the key index only gives away how the keyspace could be assigned. Plus, if at some stage there is a need to increase the key lengths to maintain security, just extend the key table with entries for the new longer keys, and then progressively update the key index field as required by a batch process (in effect decrypt with the old key and encrypt with the new key and set the key index field to

---

[17] The length in bits of the passphrase or key used to encrypt information. The longer the better. See https://www.keylength.com/en/compare/

[18] In comparison the total size of all the keys is just under 38K bytes, or not much more than a typical small image on a webpage.

[19] Classic time space trade off, it saves the need to hash the ID at each PII retrieval or update for using in this case one additional byte of storage per record.

[20] This is where a value is padded out or 'spread' over a given value space, so multiple distinct values when compressed map back to the same original values.

match). Next time there is a need to update, use the old unused key index entries.

Further, to earn bonus security points, store the keys encrypted or 'jumbled' in an undetectable way (easy with bitmapped keys), so without the right algorithm to process the keys, the keys themselves are worthless as is.

Now, some may say this is an extreme approach to take, but it has some interesting security features that make it quite attractive:

- A hacker not only has to get hold of PII data, but they also need the keys and details on the keys encryption. This significantly improves the odds of catching or identifying them and feeding them duff information (which could lead to their capture or loss of reputation).
- It 'defangs' some negative aspects of the key management problem, in that the key storage at rest is remote to the application using them. A hacker would have to compromise the service runtime to know how to decrypt the keys. This is further limited by doing the key decryption just in time, so the keys never exist in memory unencrypted (blank down after use).

Also, the early keys in the lookup table can be unencrypted and used purely for PII honeypots with a few fake records, making it even easier to detect a hacker (no real system or user should be accessing those records). In this way, stopping the hacker before they get to the real PII records.

Of course, make sure there are appropriate BCM/BCP processes around the keys as well as the PII data, with no common single point of failure; because if the keys are lost, the PII is worthless.

PII Deletion

Once done with PII and there is no longer a valid regulatory reason for keeping it, it's deleted. Do ensure the way it's deleted cannot be undone.

The reason for such 'deep' deletion is simple, as often a deletion in storage just removes the reference whilst not actually physically erasing the information. In effect where such deleted information is stored goes into a recycling list for use when more storage is required. So, until that happens, the 'deleted' PII just sits there; de-referenced but intact. If someone was to read the storage using a recovery program, they would recover the PII.

This is a real risk, hard drives that were thrown out[21] or sold in computer systems[22] have been found to hold PII.

The easiest way to prevent this is to the following prior to the deletion:

- Mark the record as deleted, using a column in the database to indicate if a record should be part of any live queries.
- Update the record with random content or use fake content encrypted with a random key that's thrown away,
- Ensure the update gets committed to storage[23].
- Clear down any buffers or caches associated with the record.

If using an archival backup service, old copies of that record will still exist in the backups until it's grandfathered away. This should not be a problem, as given the backups contain PII, they should be encrypted at rest according to these security strategies and be grandfathered away within the permitted timeframes given in the privacy policies.

If per record encryption keying has been utilised in the storage scheme, blanking down the record key makes the encrypted contents unrecoverable. Assuming such keys are distinct from the records, the keys can be 'held onto' independent of how the records get archived and delete or clear down both as independent actions as a safeguard in a failure to operate either process.

---

[21] Idaho Power Co had four hard drives sold on eBay in 2006 holding hundreds of thousands of confidential documents, employee names and SSNs and confidential memos.

[22] Loyola University disposed of a computer holding names, Social Security numbers, and financial aid information for 5800 students; before wiping the hard drive.

[23] If you are on a fault tolerant system you need to make sure all copies of the record update, which could be a challenge.

Laptops and Portable Devices

Given the amount of information loss from laptops[24] and other portable devices (such as smartphones and tablets) it's crucial to give specific attention to such devices to protect the PII that might end up on them as follows:

1. Design systems so that keep PII remote from such devices always. If PII does not need downloading, do not permit it to be.
2. If PII must exist on a portable device, it **must** be encrypted at rest always.
3. Access to the portable device is via a pin code or password always.
4. Enforce the use of strong passwords over password expiry[25].
5. The screens of mobile devices must time out and lock within 10 minutes maximum.
6. If possible, the storage of the device must be fully encrypted.
7. If possible, mobile devices **must** be configured to support remote deactivation and locking.

This way if a laptop went missing and was powered off or locked, the PII is both encrypted in of itself and in turn stored on an encrypted hard drive. This double encryption is essential, as often a laptop contains all sorts of information including access tokens and long-lived sessions that if the thief was able to access, they could then use to access the corporate systems and gain access to PII that way as well. Further, the information on the hard drive could also provide details about corporate reporting structures and contact details which would permit a social engineering attack against staff, potentially revealing yet more PII.

Remember, laptops and other portable devices will go missing or be misplaced; so, there must be in place specific policies and procedures to deal with this eventuality.

---

[24] 45% of healthcare breaches occur on stolen laptops. Verizon 2015 Data Breach Investigation Report.
[25] https://www.ncsc.gov.uk/articles/problems-forcing-regular-password-expiry

PII at the Edge

Another place to be careful about handling PII is at the edge of systems, with reference to PII 'left' on other systems and services.

For example, on a large website for every page, it goes 'Hi <firstname>' and adds onto the end of that a congratulations text if it's their birthday. The naïve way to implement is to keep going back to the database and looking up their name and date of birth for each page request; the system would soon halt. So instead put the first name and date of birth into a cookie that the browser holds and gives back with each page request. Problem solved!

The problem now is that for every user who is accessing the website puts into whatever browser they are using their first name and date of birth. Such information could be examined. Also, if the connection used to access the website isn't secure, anyone on the network in-between the browsers and website servers could easily harvest the information using packet sniffers.

For a similar reason, a smartphone application could use a long-lived API access token that also contains the user's first name and date of birth. It would suffer the same problems as the cookie. Also, applications or web apps can spin up their own local databases, which may hold PII.

A comparable situation is where a remote service keeps hold of the access token for each user that goes via it, for instance, a token that gives them access to a cloud-based unified calendar service. In this case, there is one remote system (which the business does not control) that holds lots of PII on the users.

The way to solve this is to encrypt what PII that goes into the cookie or token to make sure only the original website or service can process the PII the cookie holds.

Also, at this stage, strongly consider if such PII needs to go into the cookie or token in the first place, as other techniques (such as Edge Caching, asynchronous distributed triggering and page composition services) can give back much of the performance advantage and improve architecture qualities of the systems and services at the same time.

PII Management Frameworks

Depending on how much PII there is, and the regulatory environments expected to operate in, it may be a requirement to set up a complete Personal Information Management System (PIMS) as part of an overall compliance framework within the organisation.

Such PIMS, although not explicitly targeted to anyone regulatory framework, often do include requirements to identify legislative, regulatory and contractual requirements that relate to personal information.

A typical PIMS covers the following:

- Overarching Data Protection Policy
- Notification Procedures
- Training & Awareness Program
- Audit & Compliance Policy
- Information Management Policy
- Document & Record Control Policy
- Public Trust Charter
- Information Security Policy
- Security Policy & Procedures
- Compliance Standards
- Data Collection Procedure
- Data Quality Procedures
- Risk Management Strategy
- Data Processing Standards & Agreements
- Data Use Procedures
- Data Retention & Archive Procedures
- System/Data Specific Procedures
- Data Disposal Procedures
- Complaint Procedures
- Subject Access Procedures
- Internal Audit Procedures
- Information Notice Procedures
- Due diligence & 3rd Party audit Procedures

- 3rd Party Exchange Agreements
- Enforcement Notice Procedures

Now for a small to medium-sized business, this looks quite daunting (enough to require a Pimm's to relax), and it is, but the authoring and setting up of all these policies and procedures should only need doing once. Also, standards like BS 10012:2017[26] exist that give a framework for implementing a PIMS, so consultants and knowledgeable experts can be engaged to implement this.

Also, be aware that such PIMS tend to have quite a narrow focus on the protection of privacy, so might miss out on security requirements if PII exists across the business. This is where ISO 27001 comes in useful, by combining the two gets the best of both (in effect it fits together with the ISMS defined by ISO 27001). Also, specific regulations, like the GDPR, stipulate that organisations have:

- The ability to ensure the ongoing confidentiality, integrity, availability, and resilience of their processing systems and services;
- The ability to restore the availability of and access to personal data in a timely manner in the event of a physical or technical incident;
- A process for regularly testing, assessing and evaluating the effectiveness of technical and organisational measures for ensuring the security of the processing.

This requires a comprehensive approach to information security as well as integrating data and privacy protection into the business – so needed is a PIMS and ISO27001 to comply with the GDPR fully.

Data Loss Prevention

Now the above approach is great way to manage data privacy & security, but this needs pairing with an ability to detect & prevent PII exfiltration, done using a form of DLS (Data Loss Prevention) Software which detects potential breaches and stops them before they occur. This is achieved

---

[26] BS 10012:2017 Data Protection – Specification for a personal information management system.

using a combination of data classification, fingerprinting, monitoring and filtering.

It's important to note that DLS techniques should be considered a 'back stop', in that other techniques (such as a data flow analysis, architecture design, need to know, etc) provide structural protection to the PII – DLS on its own is not enough of a safeguard as you cannot guarantee it detects everything – remember Defence in Depth.

PII, the Office, the Cloud and Shadow IT

As hinted at previously, businesses are increasingly using SaaS providers to outsource what were internal IT systems. For the office IT manager this creates a network access & security problem, as such services need to be available from corporate networks yet be compliant with security policies. Further, employees expect access other cloud services, either for business or personal reasons – which occurs out of sight of the IT department and hence is termed Shadow IT.

Such Shadow IT creates a PII management problem, it's a vector by which PII can 'escape' easily into systems and services not under business control. Even with the best intentions concerning the security controls around your stores of PII, some manipulation outside of those stores occurs because of day to day business operations. This is also a larger IP security problem; files and documents might get shared or stolen via a Shadow IT service.

There are two solutions to this problem:

- Lockdown hard external services access and whitelist everything, or,
- Put in place policy and network management software to manage the risk for you.

The first will often result in an office riot and an ongoing headache working out what should be on the whitelist or not. It will also hasten people finding creative ways to get around the blocking (personal VPN's, private hotspots, USB thumb drives, etc.). The more enlightened approach is to manage the Shadow IT access to manage the risk and keep people happy.

In recent years a class of infrastructure has developed called a Cloud Access Security Broker (CASB). This infrastructure sits between the office and the cloud services, both those used officially by the business and the Shadow IT services. It also provides a managed gateway to either the SaaS or IaaS based services used by the business, bringing all cloud access into one management framework, regardless of from where access occurs.

With a CASB in place, the IT department can implement policies and monitoring that ensure PII and other similarly sensitive information cannot leak either by design or accident via cloud services or usage of the Internet; in effect a form of DLP.

Policy implementation uses a rules framework operating either at the network level or at a deeper application services level. It can even reach into the per-machine policies and restrict data sharing by type. The policies can even enact Information Rights Management on critical assets by a combination of usage rights and symmetric key encryption tied to an organisation, so precisely controlling who can decrypt and use the assets.

PII Rights of Usage

Before processing PII be careful it's allowed, even if anonymised, both by the terms of service, the privacy policy and the regulations in force over the business at the time. Determining this can be hard, as proof of individuals approving to the usage is required prior.

Opt-in or Opt-out

It used to be the case that a business could garner approval of usage based on an Opt-out technique, in that unless a person specifically said no to a given usage case for their PII, they had agreed to the usage by default.

Now, this is great for businesses, as there was no requirement to require approval in advance; just put a form somewhere for the individuals to use to say no and off they went. No need to notify anybody.

Of course, such ease of use became progressively increasingly abused as it was a carte-blanch to use PII in any way that suited or indeed came to mind. As a result, governments and pressure groups have responded by now requiring mandatory Opt-in and prior notification to the change in use of PII & Privacy. On the face of it for a business, this sounds like an absolute disaster, but what has happened is that such changes in usage are often 'lumped in' with a change in the overall Terms and Conditions of usage – so a failure to agree to the T&C's results in the complete product service access being disabled, not many people are going to agree to that, especially if they are paying for a service or have a lot emotionally invested in a service.

So rather than having the intended effect of giving people back control over their PII, instead they have been 'bribed' into giving away control and agreeing to PII usage not clearly understood as it's buried away in many pages of legal texts; the result is it's worse for them. Yes, they could read the Privacy Policy a new or wade through the list of changes, but when the only choice is all or nothing – few people are going to choose nothing. Although, this is changing, see the Future Trends chapter later.

Record Keeping

Yet given the above, it's now a regulatory requirement that businesses still need to prove per individual that they have given permission for the way intended to use their PII. It's usually achieved by storing in the individuals record the following:

- The precise time, to the second of when they agreed;
- Their device identifier[27] and IP used.
- What versions of the Terms & Conditions and Privacy Policy they have agreed to.

---

[27] User Agent in the case of a web browser or for a mobile phone its serial number and make.

The assumption here is that each Terms and Conditions and Privacy Policy are entirely distinct to what has gone before and always replaces the old.

Businesses often look at this with disdain, but it has two significant advantages for businesses:

- It's a positive interaction with the individual, so confirms they are still there and is a chance to upsell new products and services.
- If an individual does not respond, it can indicate that either that person is no longer interested or no longer available. So, the overall quality of the PII will go up with them suspended from use.

Also, do not make the error of considering the signing up to a product or service in of itself indicates agreement with the Privacy Policy and Terms & Conditions – make the agreement a specific recording step, which can occur within the signing up process. Remember they must have some point in the process to decline their agreement and abandon the sign-up process. If they do abandon, do not keep hold of any information they entered – they have not agreed to it.

Key Points

- Defence in Depth is complicated to get right and harder to ensure is secure the more systems and services in operation.
- The Zero Trust Model can significantly assist in reducing risks but needs using with other security techniques.
- There is no substitute for understanding hacker's motivations and the techniques they employ.
- If identifying a hacker, they can be responded to, so decreasing the likelihood of a successful attack and increasing the likelihood of them being caught.
- Avoid giving away information a hacker can use to aid their attack.
- All PII access needs logging, and in detail, so we know who accessed what and why.
- PII access logs need secure storage.

175

Personal Information Security & Systems Architecture

- All PII in transit must be over encrypted communication channels.
- Encrypt PII at rest. Be sure to use strong enough encryption and regularly review to ensure its strength.
- Cannot recover deleted PII; actively delete it.
- Be incredibly careful of laptops and portable devices.
- Watch out for PII leaking into cookies and other shared tokens.
- PII Management Frameworks provide a unified approach to how to deal with PII in the business and prove, in a regulatory sense, that appropriate actions occur.
- Do not assume the rights to PII usage, ask for them in a provable way.
- Mandatory opt-in for PII is looking to become the norm.

Chapter 10
PII Anonymisation

You have to fight for your privacy or you lose it.

Eric Schmidt

When analysing PII to discover trends or insights (or sharing it with a third party who is doing the analysis), it's required that the presentation of the data is so that it's not possible to discover the people whom the analysis is based upon on. Especially if communicating the results of that analysis publicly. It could also be the analysis itself is one of a sensitive nature (medical or financial come to mind) which regardless of careful analysis and comparison with other datasets do not reveal who the individuals are.

The principal way to protect individual's identities in such situations is by the process of anonymization. This chapter will explore this subject in detail and explain the approved ways of achieving anonymization as well as some of the traps if not applied correctly.

Note: Given the highly technical and mathematical nature of this process, a requirement is a technical background to get the best out of this chapter.

Ensuring Anonymisation is Strong Enough

The aim of anonymisation is that for a given anonymised dataset is it not possible with any degree of confidence to rediscover the individuals it's

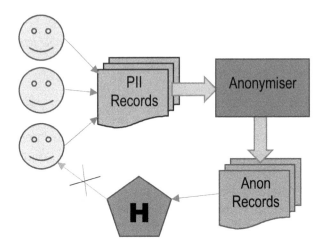

Figure 11 - the Process of Anonymisation

based off. Demonstrated with the diagram below.

As shown we have three individuals who have records containing PII, these records pass through an Anonymiser process producing the now green Anonymised records stripped of their PII. What should not happen is that a bad actor (like the red cybercriminal shown above) is able to manipulate and analyse the Anonymised records to rediscover the individuals (or even one individual as shown), as then the Anonymiser has failed to do its job of protecting the identities.

Therefore, anonymisation can only be successful if the reduction of identifying information in the data set is to the degree that each record is identical to at least one or more other records (safety in numbers approach, individuals have become anonymous groups). This is known as the k-anonymity principal.

> A data release has the k-anonymity property if the information for each person in the release cannot be distinguished from at least k-1 individuals whose information also appears in the release. In effect, everyone is in groups of at least k individuals per group.
> https://epic.org/privacy/reidentification/Sweeney_Article.pdf

Below are the techniques to enact such anonymisation.

Anonymisation Techniques

To achieve the right level of anonymisation the various techniques described below get combined.

Attribute Suppression

Attribute suppression is the removal of an entire bit of data or column in a dataset. Done either when the attribute isn't required in the anonymised dataset, or other anonymisation techniques do not sufficiently anonymise it. This is by far the most reliable anonymisation technique as there is no way to recover something that isn't there.

By way of example, you have a set of records as follows:

Name	Age	Married	Credit Rating
Fred Blogs	54	Yes	AA
David Rich	43	Yes	B
John Jones	39	No	C

By removing the Name column, we effectively make the set of records anonymous.

Age	Married	Credit Rating
54	Yes	AA
43	Yes	B
39	No	C

Without the name column, each row could refer to potentially many individuals, assuming there is no other context to this table (see later).

Record Suppression

Record suppression is the removal of entire records from the dataset. This removes records that are unique and do not meet anonymisation criteria such as k-anonymity. It's crucial that the deletion is permanent and not just hidden, it really needs to be not there in the resultant data set.

Character Masking

This is where the actual characters of a data value changes to mask or hide what the original characters where (e.g. 10245 becomes 10***). Masking is usually partial and not applied to all the characters in some attribute.

Do be careful with masking, as sometimes the length and combination of what's masked could be used as an aid with another data to reveal what was masked. The way around this is either stagger the masking lengths (so 10245 still becomes 10*** but so does 102456) or introduce a random element to the length of the mask Also be careful of checksums on the data; this might allow some recovery of other parts of the masked data.

Pseudonymization

Pseudonymization replaces fields holding the most personal identifying information with artificial identifiers (known as pseudonyms).

So typically, this is mapping some form of personal identification into another 'namespace' as a pseudonym and is it not clear from knowledge of the pseudonym to which individual the information relates to.

The advantage here is that we know the mapping, so if later we need to get back to the individual, say giving the pseudonymised information to a marketing research agency who then profiled it looking for new leads, we can do so. Indeed, this is one of the key benefits of pseudonymization it is possible to hand off such data to a third party without risk of that party incurring a breach that causes the revealing of identities.

How the mapping's done is using one of two types of technique:

- **Randomly generated** – generate a distinct random identifier per individual.
- **Algorithmically derived** – based on the information in the record. Hashing or cryptographically encoding a unique identifier is a standard technique.

Whether randomly generated, or generated by a hash, when the mapping needs reversing, a mapping needs maintaining in a table. If using a cryptographic technique, then we just keep safe the key used.

Given the mapping or the key is critical to the Pseudonymization technique, it is vital they are secure and are only used by those authorised.

Here is a trap with pseudonymisation that one must be careful of, as the ability to hide the individual strongly depends on the information as a whole not being combined with other data sets to reveal the individual. For instance, given a record as follows:

Name	Fred Jones
Sex	Male
Date of Birth	3/5/75
Address	10 Wild Place, Outback 34532
Yearly Income	$100,000
Credit Rating	AA

And pseudonymised it as follows:

ID	X08655
Sex	Male
Date of Birth	3/5/75
Zip Code	34532
Yearly Income	$100,000
Credit Rating	AA

We have also realised the address could be a bit of a privacy give away, so just allowed through the zip code. On the face of it, this looks like it cannot get back to the individual, yet knowledge of a person's Sex, Date of Birth and Zip code (in the USA at least) gives a strong odds-on chance of finding the person. So, if a database existed that provided the mapping, the pseudonymisation is reversible in the majority case.

The trouble is, when making available such pseudonymised data sets, there isn't prior knowledge of what datasets are out there or can be made available as required (or indeed combined with other data sets to provide more means to reverse the anonymisation). So, the tendency is to err on the side of caution and be especially careful with attributes that could be indexed for other data sets be suitably anonymised as well.

Another problem to keep in mind is if reusing the anonymisation mapping in other data releases, then the resultant ID's can be used as a common key to combining data releases, which could enable rediscovery of the individuals.

The GDPR regulations have recognised these problems with pseudonymised data and have stated[1]:

> *"Personal data which have undergone pseudonymisation, which could be attributed to a natural person by the use of additional information should be considered to be information on an identifiable natural person."*

So, with respect to Europe at least, if there isn't 100% confidence that the pseudonymised data cannot refer to an individual in a way out of business control – such data is still within the remit of the GDPR as PII.

Generalisation

Generalisation (or recoding) is when there is a deliberate reduction in data precision. For example:

- Converting a precise location to a general location,
- Converting an age in an age range,
- Converting a Date of Birth into an age.
- Converting a weight into a weight range, etc

---

[1] Recital 26

The reduction in the precision needs to be enough to anonymise yet not too much to make the final data useless. Also, be aware that the outliers in a data range (those that lie to the top and bottom) might need to be part of a larger range to ensure they are part of a group of anonymised individuals (so the fact they are alone at the extremes cannot aid discovery of who they are).

Swapping

Swapping (or shuffling or permutation) is the rearrangement of data such that individual attribute values are still present, but they do not correspond to the original records. Typically performed when the analysis only needs to look at the aggregated data or at per attribute level; so, the relationship between the attributes at a record level does not matter.

Data Perturbation

Data perturbation is the modification of the values in the original dataset to be slightly different, thereby breaking the exact one to one correspondence with the original data.

This 'fudges' quasi-identifiers (such as numbers and dates) that could be used with other data sources to reveal identity. Use this technique where data accuracy isn't critical.

Such perturbation occurs by:

- **Rounding** – reducing the number of significant digits or to the closest value.
- **Random noise** – adding an amount of random noise to a value.

It's essential that the degree of perturbation be proportional to the range of values in an attribute. Too small, the anonymisation effect will be weak; too much and it impacts the usefulness of the dataset.

Also, be aware that a series of perturbed values that refer to the same action or event, saying a GPS path of an individual commuting over many days, could have their start and end points averaged together to reveal the precise location of someone's home and place of work (or even their favourite café). Work needs doing in these cases to ensure it's not easy to reverse the perturbing[2].

Adding randomness to the data is a form of differential privacy[3], where through the right level of added randomness the presence (or not) of a given individual cannot be determined with useful confidence.

Data Aggregation

Data aggregation is where instead of giving a list of records provide just the summarised values. This technique is only applicable when just the aggregated data is enough.

As for how to do the summarization, that depends upon the end usage case, and there are multiple statistical techniques which are appropriate.

Although do be careful to check for groups having too few records after aggregation, as this could reveal an individual either directly (a grouping that contains just one record can be directly mapped to an individual with ease, known as an External Attack) or inference from knowledge of the membership of the rest of the group[4]. Therefore, after aggregation, it's usual to check for such groups and suppress them.

Also, watch out for individuals who over contribute to the aggregation compared to others in the dataset. Such individuals can infer information about others from the summation. For instance, given a table of total incomes per town, for one town an individual contributes most of the income, so that individual knows everybody else is contributing little. This is known as a Dominance Attack.

Also, remember it doesn't have to be the individual who enacts the attack, it could be a third party with knowledge of the individual.

---

[2] Identify revisited locations and ensure the same perturbing value applies across the set.
[3] https://en.wikipedia.org/wiki/Differential_privacy
[4] An average measure across two values will, if one value is known, allow calculation of the other. Likewise, for a group of 3 values, knowing 2 allows calculation of the unknown value and so on for larger groups. This is known as an Internal Attack.

Anonymisation Process

Below is a suggested process for performing anonymisation on a dataset.

#1 The Release Model

The anonymised dataset can usually be released in two ways, either Public or Non-public. Public refers to making the dataset available to anyone, and Non-public refers to a release to a known set of recipients. Releasing to the public is the more challenging of the two as you have little control over the data usage or analysis, anything could happen.

#2 Acceptable Re-identification Risk Threshold

Work out the risk of re-identification the business is prepared to carry given the release model, and the expected use cases and the degree of control maintained over its usage.

#3 Classify Attributes

Classify the attributes in the dataset as either direct identifiers, indirect identifiers or non-identifiers.

#4 Remove Unused Attributes

Remove any attributes not required for the use cases at this stage.

#5 Anonymise Direct and Indirect Identifiers

Using the techniques described previously anonymise everything but the non-identifiers. Also, check for the need to suppress any outlier records.

#6 Check Risk Against the Threshold

Work out if the anonymisation performed so far is sufficient and apply more anonymisation until within your agreed threshold.

#7 Evaluate the Solution

Check if what's left of the dataset is sufficient to meet the goals or utility of the use cases. If unable to meet the goals, either the process of anonymisation will need performing differently, or the dataset cannot be suitably anonymised for the use cases envisaged.

#8 Controls

Work out the security and operational controls required to release the anonymised data set and be secure.

#9 Document

Ensure the process of anonymisation is well documented and kept secure; this aids with reviews and any fine-tuning that may be required in the future.

Anonymous References

It could be that there is a requirement to communicate a reference to an individual or a set of individuals through an otherwise insecure or less trusted third party. The goal is to communicate such references without giving away who the individuals are.

This case tends to crop up when requiring a third party to keep track of an individual yet not know whom that person is based on information given to them. For instance, tracking their usage of a third-party website or service.

On the face of it, this looks like pseudonymization, but the reference often needs to be long-lived and globally unique to that individual. In that, it's passed around and used as a surrogate by the third party with ease. Further, the reference in of itself should say nothing about number, order or age of the individual records kept, it should convey no more information than just being a simple anonymous reference.

Luckily there exists a data type almost designed for this very purpose, namely the GUID, which is an acronym for 'Globally Unique Identifier' and is a standards-based data type. It consists of a 128-bit number generated in such a way that it's very highly likely to be globally unique if everybody uses the same method of GUID generation.

The beauty of GUID's in this case is:

- The GUID in of itself conveys no information[5].
- Multiple machines can generate GUID's at the same time with no risk of collisions[6].
- The namespace of GUID's is large, so attempting to 'fish' via GUID's for matching records is inherently infeasible if using protections against denial of service or dictionary attacks.
- GUID's are a known entity in the software industry.

Do note when using GUID's it's vital that:

- All the programs generating GUID's generate the same version of GUID, so guaranteeing behaviour.
- Before usage do check that it's unique against the records. Glitches do occur and better to safeguard against them. The cost should be cheap, as already indexed are the GUID's. Plus, if the GUID column is uniquely indexed a dupe is not allowed, although if on distributed storage this may not be enforceable at that level.

Data Mining

A related case to anonymous references is when PII is fed into a Data Mining service, again GUID's can be used to carry through a reference, but what goes into the Data Mine needs careful screening to prevent rediscovery, or it will be classed as PII again (see the GDPR, which can create an erasure problem under the Right to be forgotten).

---

[5] Version 1 does encode the date-time and MAC address, so can be a privacy leak.
[6] Using versions 1 and 2. Version 4 has a 50% probability of a collision once 2.71 quintillion GUID's are generated.

Also, the ethics of doing this needs careful consideration and must be a factor in deciding what degree of personal information feeds into the Data Mine and the amount of anonymisation undertaken.

Merging Problems

As previously hinted before, releasing (and especially those publicly) any anonymised dataset runs the risk of cross-indexing with other datasets to establish who the individuals are. Even if they fail in discovering the individuals, the number of attributes per anonymous person increases after such a merge – so yet more valuable analysis can occur on the increased dataset. Such extended analysis could be well beyond what's allowed or expected for each of the datasets on their own, and there is no way of knowing its occurring.

Further depending on the structure of the dataset and what's in each attribute, it's possible to establish complex relationships between the records (such as dependency, tree or graph structures), using them to merge in additional datasets that exhibit matching structures.

It's also possible to apply probabilistic techniques to establish relationships between records that have no unique identifiers or are affected by errors (Fellegi-Sunter & Jaro, 2014). This technique is known as Record Linkage (RL)[7].

Business Sensitive Enumeration

An aspect rarely covered concerning anonymisation is that the data can 'leak' sensitive information about the source business by accident. For instance, an anonymised table of all the customers of a business directly counts the number of customers that business has.

---

[7] https://en.wikipedia.org/wiki/Record_linkage

To avoid this problem either the dataset is just as a representative sample or it's a summary view from which establishing the source quantity is not possible. If required, the dataset could be 'padded out' to hide any sensitive business dimensions.

Targeting Problems

A related problem to maintaining anonymisation occurs with targeted advertising, namely given enough segmentation controls over a targeted user demographic dataset it's possible to discover individuals or minority groups through cross-correlation[8].

This is an interesting problem as advertisers want to target precisely to maximise their returns, yet the very act of precision targeting runs the risk of privacy breach. To address this problem needs a combination of restrictions around the degree of combined precision related to selected group size and diversity; with improved regulations and visibility.

Key Points

- PII Anonymization allows 3rd parties to analyse PII without knowing whom it refers to.
- The anonymisation needs to be strong enough not to allow its reversal and the individual's rediscovery.
- There are several techniques that when combined can ensure strong anonymisation.
- GUID's provide a handy way to share a reference to an individual without giving away their identity to a 3rd party.
- Be aware of the risks posed to anonymisation by other data sets merged with them to reveal identities.

---

[8] https://arxiv.org/abs/1803.10099

Chapter 11
Putting it all Together

Eventually, all things merge into one, and a river runs through it.

Norman Maclean

Now that you have worked out precisely what PII the business has and where it is and its value, now is the time to look at how to bring all that PII together and to extract it from the other systems.

This is a critical step as possibly many systems are relieved of their burden of having to store PII, and this will need carefully made changes. In return, the PII ends up in one or two systems, and it's much easier to put in place the right controls & procedures around such a small number of systems.

It's essential at this stage that all PII goes through the same merging process, as it's the only way of getting certainty that all the information on an individual is known and associated to that individual. Otherwise, there is a risk of information going missing, which affects the ability to comply with access regulations and security requirements (it could 'escape').

In this chapter, the focus is on the data processing aspects of this step to get the information into an appropriate storage system and the processes and procedures which go with that. The next chapter focusses on the actual implementation and operational challenges of creating a PII store or vault.

Merging Strategy

First off, take the PII analysis and work out exactly the PII records required. It might be that all the distinct pools of PII in the systems join

191

into one big record set using a universally guaranteed identifier. In that everyone's information merges and deduplicated across the source systems to create one PII record per individual in the vault.

Although in practice this rarely happens, as even within a single dataset duplication or partial duplication can occur – it all comes down to the degree of effort undertaken in keeping the information clean and correct over time.

It's crucial at this stage to only consider systems that are original sources of PII; they shouldn't be straight copies of PII from other systems, they must be contributing something distinct to the process otherwise running the risk of either doing too much work or introducing noise sources that make combining the data more difficult.

Step#1: Uniform Transformation

Depending on the amount of variation in information across the contributing source systems, one can either have a straightforward time merging the data or an absolute nightmare. It all comes down to how carefully defined the various fields of information are and how consistent they are within and across systems. Take for instance a date; represented as:

- 1/12/81
- 12/1/81
- 12/1/1981
- 1st December 1981

Which creates a problem, is it the 1st December 1981 or the 12th January 1981? This all comes down to the precision of the representation of the date in this case. A similar problem exists with names:

- Fred Blogss
- F. Bloggs
- Bloggs, F.
- Bloggs, Fred A

Now if someone has a double-barrelled surname, things really become fun depending on the storage of the first, middle and last names. So again, the precision of representation is vital. Therefore, always pick a target representation that gives the most chance of preserving information in its most complete form without variation.

Some data types to be particularly careful with:

- **Money** – needs storing in a form that does not lose precision, i.e. decimal with a fixed number of digits after the decimal point. Also, ensure to store the currency if the system deals with multiple currencies.
- **Date** – not only does there to be agreement on the format of the date, but is there also a requirement to know which time zone it relates to?
- **Time** – again agree on the format and store the time zone to which it relates (plus convert to UTC[1]).
- **Distances/Lengths/Weights/Volumes/etc.** – the unit of measurement must be consistent[2].

To keep a grip on this and avoid having to deal with each situation per system, we suggest the following:

1. Decide on an intermediate format or store to write the various records of PII to, say an XML format or dedicated database. Of course, all in a suitably secured environment or within the footprint of the intended PII vault deployment. Where possible preserve any modification or creation timestamp information, this will help working out later how fresh the information is. Also, each record must have an identifier that references back to the source record.
2. Develop tools which read these formats and based on a field format dictionary[3] converts each record on the following basis:

---

[1] UTC – Coordinated Universal Time.
https://en.wikipedia.org/wiki/Coordinated_Universal_Time
[2] NASA lost its $125-million Mars Climate Orbiter because spacecraft engineers failed to convert from English to metric measurements when exchanging vital data before the craft was launched (Oct 1999).
[3] Per type of field what its well-formed format is which is globally consistent across the

  a. All fields of a known format, convert and write to the success file

  b. Otherwise, write to the check file.

3. Examine records in the check file and if fixable put back into the conversion tool.

At the end of this per system is a success file containing all the PII ready to merge per system.

Step#2: Group Records per Individual

This is where what appropriate linking strategy for duplicate entries on individuals is determined. In an ideal world, all records will be perfect dupes. But, if there isn't a global update policy to keep the information in sync across systems, it's highly likely the records will differ. This difference in records needs dealing with, as it must be determined which records hold the most accurate information.

The merging problem splits into two problems:

- Identifying the records related to each individual and group them.
- Merging the groups of records into one that preserves the most information.

It could be there is a global identifier for individuals that exist across all the sources systems; it's then used to group the records. Although this is usually not the case, then what fields together are likely to give a unique enough key to avoid merging the wrong people together needs determining.

Surrogate Keying

This is where a single field or a set of fields create a surrogate key. The fields chosen depend upon:

- The consistency of format and accuracy of a field;
- How up to date the field is,
- If it's extensively filled in, ideally in all records, and,

business.

- A broad range of values.

The goal here is to have one or two fields which can be 'trusted' that will provide a reliable surrogate key. Candidates include:

- Telephone number,
- Email address,
- Date of Birth,
- Account number

The Full Name may be included, but only if there is high confidence of consistency of format for all contributing records, otherwise 'F. Bloggs' and 'Fred Bloggs' won't match. Do not make use of the full address for similar noise reasons (unless it's transformed into a geolocation and that's used instead).

Note: it's also perfectly acceptable to create more than one surrogate key, with lower or different requirements of uniqueness.

Now using the most specific or accurate surrogate key first identify the sets of records for which 2 or more keys are identical. These record groups you put aside for later merging. Now repeat group identification with the next most specific key and keep setting aside what's found.

At the end of this should be records that consist of:

- Individuals who uniquely only existed on one system, or,
- Individuals whose information was so varied they cannot be safely automatically grouped.

This final list of unmerged records will require manual techniques to work out if any merge groups can be established. Also, at this stage determine if certain records need throwing away due to inferior quality or being very much out of date (not permitted to keep).

Fuzzy Hashing

If it's hard grouping records together it's likely because of high levels of diversity in the underlying records; there is no one proper surrogate key available. This is where fuzzy hashing comes in useful.

A fuzzy hash (more formally known as Context Triggered Piecewise Hashes (CTPH)) is a hash which hashes with similar value for similar inputs, which are compared to determine the degree of matching. In this way, those records which are similar can be identified as being homologies of each other and hence good candidates for grouping. Programs like ssdeep[4] can be the basis for implementation but do be careful to confirm the scoring thresholds are set sufficiently high to avoid false matches.

Step#3: Merge Each Record Group

Compared to grouping, merging is usually easier and goes as follows:

1. Establish an order between the records based on when last updated and if the source systems are 'trusted' or not[5]. With recently updated and most trusted on top. Those records which do not have an update time or come from untrusted systems go on the bottom.
2. Working from the bottom of the list to the top create a record by overwriting values per field that came before. Unknown or blank fields do not overwrite what came before.

In this way, merging is by confidence in the data source and preserves any values only known by a subset of systems.

Remember, the merging is just purely for PII fields, all the other none PII fields remain in the donating systems. It's also assumed that there is no critical dependency between any of the PII fields (other than the individual), so merging per field is safe.

Record Referencing

By now there is a definitive list of records that are to go into the store. Remember part of the 'deal' of the PII going into the store is external systems which need access have it, so they require a reference to keep. Do this by generating a GUID per record for internal references and give that

---

[4] https://ssdeep-project.github.io/ssdeep/index.html
[5] Trusted in this context refers to if the source system had known good data keeping and maintenance techniques, or if they were core to the data processing in the business. The trusted ordering can be determined off line first.

to the contributing systems to keep in replace of the PII they have deleted once the store is up and running.

With the contributing systems (plus those with PII copies that need to go as well) take a stepping stone approach, as follows:

1. Have them code in a configuration switch to turn on referencing the PII via the GUID from the store. For now, it's off.
2. Get them to store the GUIDs in their records correctly.
3. Flick the configuration switch to use the store and confirm operation using the test to production release process (no hiccups in production please)
4. Once live, actively blank down the PII holding fields in the systems now in the store and then remove them from the schemas with their supporting code.
5. Actively confirm the clear down is complete and that PII is no longer showing up in the systems.

There is a big assumption here, which is since taking the PII for merging and the systems operating, the data has not diverged. If divergence is a concern, either add a step where the contributing systems both write to the store as well as write to their storage (respecting record modification when importing to the store from the merge); or, perform an additional merging run using all the records updated since the first merge. Given this problem, most IT departments would do the changeover out of normal business hours if they have the option to do so.

Another alternative is to have a per record 'migrated' switch that controls usage of the PII store. This way the changeover batches per record per system and built-in checks ensure use of the up to date information. This avoids the need for a 'big bang' approach to the migration and therefore no downtime.

Storage Functions

Depending on the complexity of how PII is utilised storage can go from a basic record that supports CRUD (Create, Read, Update and Delete) operations to something cross-indexed with real-time updating to an in-house data mining system. Fortunately, these functions can layer on as shown below.

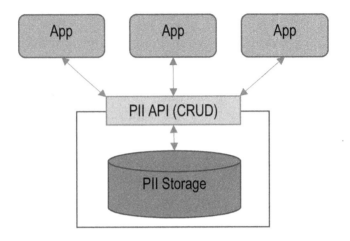

In the set up above the PII Store is extremely basic and acts as a simple 'card' store, in that Apps can only manipulate single records with no reference to any other record. Apps can only see the PII records via the PII API which implements CRUD operations; there are no other means of access open to them. The disadvantage of this approach is that discovery or searching for a record via its PII isn't supported, the Apps may have a way to find a record using some other identifier (say account number) but anything relating to PII (such as a name or address) isn't possible (or not practically effective).

Also remember that in the PII store, the unique handle to each record is via a GUID generated only by the PII store.

So, the next step up in functionality is to include some PII indexes, as follows:

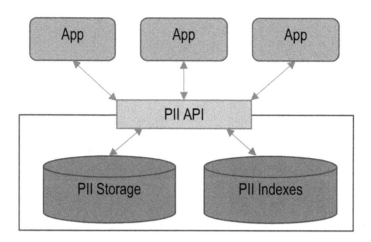

In such a set-up, searching by the PII that's indexed is now possible. In effect, the API gains some search methods and is no longer pure CRUD in operation; making the system a lot more practical. Be careful that the mechanism of searching cannot enumerate all the PII Records with ease (get all records with a surname beginning with A, then B, then C, etc.).

Data Subject Access Requests

However, wait, we have forgotten something! In most regulatory environments, a data subject (individual) has the right to access the PII held on their behalf and can either correct or demand its deletion. This is known as a Subject Access Request (SAR).

Further such requests need answering within a specific timeframe, for instance for a business:

- **GDPR** – provide access within one month with the option of making the requests electronically, and you cannot charge for it usually. Access ideally should be to a secure remote system where they can see their information[6].
- **Australia Privacy Act** – provide access within 30 days in the manner requested by the individual if reasonable and practicable to do so, and you cannot charge for access.
- **Canada Privacy Act** – provide access within 30 days either by paper copy, remote access, or direct access (on premises). Can charge a minimal fee to just cover costs.

So, this results in the following system design:

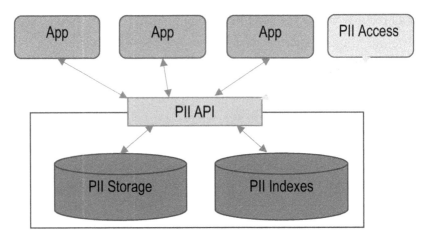

---

[6] Recital 63 EU GDPR

The PII Access app is a secured app by which authenticated and authorised individuals can see all the PII held on them and correct as required (or request its deletion). The PII API requires a unique set of entry points to manage such access, do not just bolt it onto an existing application as it needs specific security controls as the whole PII Record is recovered. Also, the Data Subject needs the ability to download a dump of their data in a standard format to permit its transfer to another party if they wish to be forgotten.

Make sure to:

- Use at least a 2FA technique to verify their identity.
- Remember in handling a request to cover paper-based records as well (hence why it's important to get all PII into the store, as this is slow).
- Redact information relating to other individuals.
- Check if exemptions apply to certain classes of data.
- Be prompt in handling such requests.
- Log the access request, the availability of the information, its notification and the information access (all in the store), so proving compliance.

Data Subject Processing Restriction

Under the GDPR a Data Subject has the right to have the processing of their data restricted, in that once enacted you can only store their data and not do any active processing or usage of the data[7].

To implement this, create a Restricted flag against all individual records of PII that are directly associated back to an individual. This either means implementing a single flag in their primary record (referenced back to from each secondary record) or propagate the flag into the secondary records to help with performance. Then in the PII Access app implement a form to request restriction activation so the Data Subject can detail why they want it restricted, depending on the level of restriction required (partial or whole) this form could be processed automatically, or go right to the nominated Data Controller representative for immediate action.

---

[7] https://advisera.com/eugdpracademy/gdpr/right-to-restriction-of-processing/

201

Given such a Restricted flag assists with freezing data in legal investigations and other operational cases (for instance a hacking incident), it's useful to implement regardless.

PII Sharing

Now the above situations operate in a PII vacuum, in that PII not shared with any other business in any form (anonymised or not). What would happen if the business were to be part of a data brokering arrangement? Let's see.

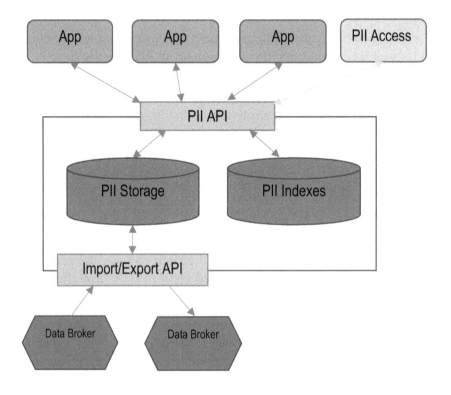

Now this usage case becomes interesting if covered by the GDPR in Europe. Depending where the Data Brokers are (i.e. are they covered by the GDPR as well) the business may not be permitted to take information from a Data Broker or give information to a Data Broker, even if the data in of itself isn't PII (i.e. it could be combined with other data the Broker has to become PII).

Now if all consents have been granted from the data subjects in question, record the sharing of data in accordance with the regulations[8]. Although, as of writing, precisely who must get permission for the Data Brokers is still a grey area.

It's important to note that if a Data Subject requests to be forgotten, then if sharing their data with 3rd parties, then the 3rd parties need to be notified to forget it as well. Similarly, if they wish to restrict the data processing, this needs propagating to the 3rd parties as well.

---

[8] https://gdpr-info.eu/art-30-gdpr/

Anonymised Data Mining

Now, what about the case where the business wants to share anonymised

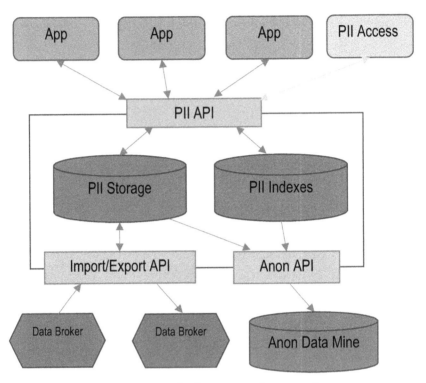

data with other parties, say a marketing research agency?

In this case, an Anonymous Data Mine or dump is generated for marketing research purposes, so the business can get a better understanding of its customers via a 3rd party marketing research agency who uses the Data Mine provided to with. In this way the business complies with the regulations as the 3rd party will not be able to reverse the anonymisation to get back to the individuals in question.

The Anon API makes sure the data requested is irreversible by only supplying a set of pre-configured views into the data. Trying to programmatically determine if what's being requested can be safely anonymised isn't proveably safe.

Also, to protect against the combining of the various Data Mines to cause re-identification, either:

- Do not supply the GUID's for the individuals in the export,
- Map the GUID's for individuals through a unique namespace per Data Mine, or,
- Map each field per individual through its own GUID namespace, thereby breaking the data per person row integrity.

What's considered appropriate will depend on the amount of data, it's sensitivity, and the degree of trust placed with the 3rd party agency.

It's important to note that the ability of GUID's (and similarly manufactured tokens) to 'hide' yet reference out of sight data is nothing new. In effect secondary or foreign keying in a database maintains a relationship without giving away what is on either end – you query the tables concerned to find out what information is associated along that relationship.

Change Notification

It's quite likely that a change in a PII Record is an event that contributing applications and services would be interested in knowing about. For instance, if a PII Record expires and self-erases then other systems should not be maintaining a GUID reference to what's now a non-existent record, this could lead to errors or inconsistent behaviours.

There are two principal ways in which such event notification occurs:

- **Message Busses** – messages exchanged using a pub/sub model along with a reliable transport.
- **Web Hooks** – the remote systems are called to tell them about the event, using a reliable queuing service (maybe a private message bus) to ensure such notifications are always made.

The alternative to doing this is to provide a 'get events' endpoint in the PII store API. The only trouble with this is:

- The PII store must maintain state on which system is interested in which event and keep a record if each system has seen such an event. This can become quite expensive.
- Each system needs to keep calling this endpoint to find out if anything of interest has occurred – which does not scale well.

On anything but a trivial setup polling for events can be very inefficient. Given the range of technologies available now for message queuing and dispatch[9], this will be a more natural route to take.

So, assuming the message bus solution is used, the system diagram now

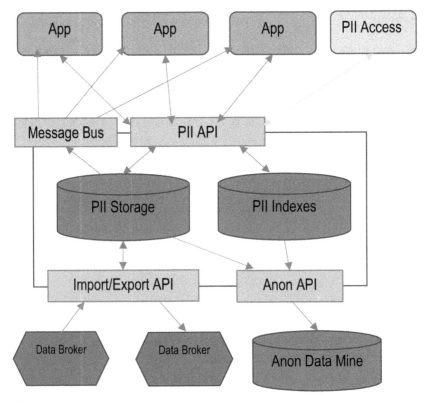

looks like.

---

[9] https://www.rabbitmq.com/ , AWS SNS

In the above diagram, the message bus is something closely tied to the PII store, but it does not have to be this way, there could well be an existing shared message bus service that the store just contributes into as required.

Note: Remember no PII can be sent over the notification, it can certainly indicate what fields have changed, just not their content. Unless there is end-to-end encryption and only the specific applications can pick up the messages.

Transborder Transfers

Europe isn't the only region or country to have strict Transborder data exchange requirements. Some form of control or record is required when PII is transferred between different regions and regulatory scopes. This implies the need to keep a record per PII of:

- **Where it came from** – was it internally sourced or provided via a 3rd party?
- **Where it went** – was it shared with a 3rd party and when?
- **What security controls are in place** – was it encrypted and what security measurements does the 3rd party have?

Regardless of where those other 3rd parties were. Reason being regulations do change over time and what was in or out of scope changes as a result. The business does **not** want to be caught in the situation of not knowing enough about the PII to be unable to make a safe determination. Consider this a form of PII Meta Data or Logging that exists alongside the PII in the store. We go into more detail on this next.

Remember the business is legally responsible for PII and needs to be able to prove they have the right permissions and consent to be able to use it.

PII Meta Data

As discussed before, PII cannot be used in a vacuum; there is a lot of additional contextual information required to ensure a business can legally manipulate PII in the way allowed. This creates somewhat of a problem, as PII regulations keep evolving, so what in addition needs keeping?

A business needs to keep the following PII Meta Data:

- Where the PII came from.
- When created and last updated.
- Who the PII was shared directly with and when.
- What can be done with it and when those rights expire.
- When the PII itself expires.

Now, this may look like a lot of information, but it should not be a significant amount to keep. The important thing is it's queried as needed, so a PII Meta Data Index needs to be created. Let's extend the system diagram.

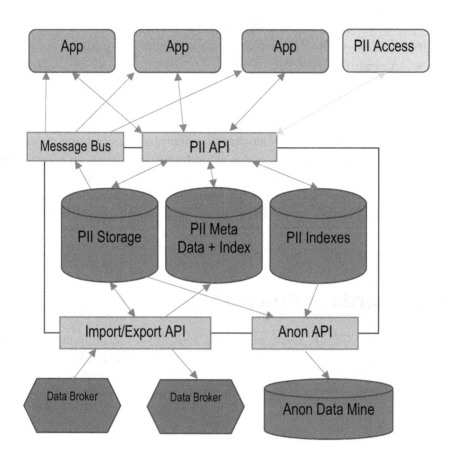

In the diagram, the PII Meta Data is in its storage with its own index so that it can scale apart from the PII Storage. Also, in of itself, it's not PII, this avoids 'polluting' the real PII Storage with none PII data. This also means the metadata can be versioned independently of the PII.

This also means housekeeping queries can run across the PII Meta Data, for instance:

- Locating PII that might be too old to be current and flagging for validation;
- Locating PII that is about to expire and flagging for permission renewal by contacting the individual;

209

- Locating PII that has expired and ensuring it's deleted;
- Finding all the PII permitted to share with a 3rd party;
- Age profiling the PII.

All this can be done *without* impacting the day to day operation of the rest of the system.

It's also important to remember that fine grain permissions and expiry will need to be 'carried' with PII that is shared with 3rd parties. In effect when the right of usage expires the remote copy a 3rd party has should also expire of its own accord at near the same time. Therefore, when sharing a PII record in addition to the PII holding fields supply the expiry details as well.

PII Records of Processing

Under the EU GDPR and other regulations, it's a requirement of a Data Controller and Data Processor to keep records of what data processing occurred to the PII and the handling of the processing results. Keep these records with the PII Meta Data as shown below.

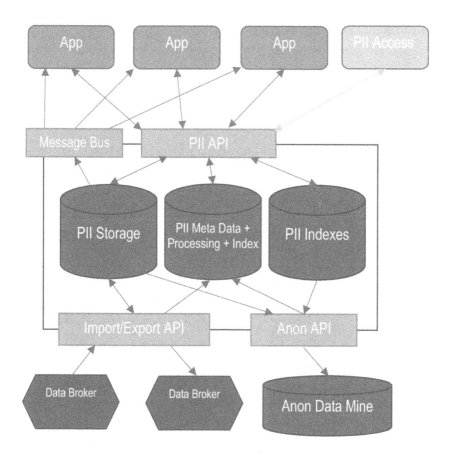

The records that need keeping are at least:

- Name or contact details of any controller, processor or officers involved;
- The purposes of the processing per specific controller;
- A description of the categories of data subjects and categories of personal data involved (references);
- Categories of recipients of the personal data including third-party countries or international organisations;
- Identification of any third parties receiving personal data and security safeguards employed in transfer;

- Where available the envisaged time limits for the erasure of different categories of data;
- General description of the technical and organisational security measures in force.

Note: we have included a link between the Anon API and the Meta Data store as it is good practice to log all processing (even that producing anonymised results). All PII sourced result data that goes out should do so with a processing record (including to Data Brokers). We would recommend doing this even if you are an SMB ordinarily exempt from such record keeping[10].

The implementation of such record keeping will have to support searching, reporting and exporting the processing records as required in response to regulatory requests; with suitable security controls. As an aid to management of data processing the creation or modification of a data processing record should produce a notification to the manager in charge of the data processing. Also, prohibit the deletion of data processing records at a fundamental level (i.e. the database account cannot perform deletion).

Also, certain regulations (Switzerland) require notification to the overseeing body prior to the start of data processing. This will require implementation of a notification flag and a 'Go/No Go' status flag with the processing record. In fact, it might be advantageous to implement versioning of the processing record to record adherence to process.

Access Controls and Limits

A subject area not touched on yet is how access control is enforced and how limits are set on the amount of PII that's accessed to ensure PII isn't being 'lifted' out of systems by bad actors. Remember PII breaches can occur either via external actors (cybercriminals) or internal actors

---

[10]   https://iapp.org/resources/article/the-eu-general-data-protection-regulation/#A30 A30 clause 5.

(employees), so the approach to security with the store must cover off both these cases. Key to this is how access control works in practice.

System/User Access Control

Just as it's essential to know who is accessing the PII Store, it's vital to know via what they are accessing. These two facts together determine the environment in which the PII action occurs. For instance, what about the following two cases:

- **Case A** - Customer Care User X accesses the PII Store from their machine in the office,
- **Case B** – Customer Care User X accesses the PII Store via their machine at their home.

Case A looks like a valid case, while Case B could be a bit fishy. Therefore, where someone accesses PII from or via is just as important as who they are. So as a result, the Authorisation system needs to be taking this into account.

Something else to consider in the AuthZ model is the time of access as well, and if time zones need considering. This is where frameworks like the Zero Trust Networking model could come in useful, as that mandates access by system and user and requires encryption in all cases as networking is untrusted.

Usage limits and Counting

It's also essential there are controls per period over PII access in volume. For instance, allowing a Customer Care account access to a single PII record once a minute on average during office hours with a maximum of 480 records per day. Without such a control, if a hacker was to take over the Customer Care account, they could script it to pull down all the PII records in quick order. With the limits in place, access would be blocked, and an alert sent out.

The trick is to find a balance between what's acceptable usage and when the block comes into force.

One thing to be incredibly careful of is making sure the block user account sharing, we suggest all user accounts that have access to PII implement 2FA[11]. Further, limit each account to one current session at the time (more and the oldest current session drops), then there is no benefit sharing accounts.

Utilising PII Value

Something else to be aware of is that all PII isn't equal in value and this is indeed known by the hacker or a bad actor. An added way to enforce usage limits is to limit the amount of PII Value accessed in a given time. This has the lovely advantage that if the PII accessed isn't consistent; you can be sure the controls maintain the appropriate degree of protection.

To implement this per role provide two additional PII value limits as follows:

- Maximum per field PII Value
- Maximum per record total PII Value

So, if given a Customer Care Role as follows:

- Max per Field = 4
- Max per Record = 8
- Daily limit = 480

Then that CC role can only see in any PII Record the following:

- Full Name, email address, home number and address, OR,
- Full Name, email address and date of birth.
- Full Name, home address and date of birth.

Based on the PII Values given in Table 1 Chapter 6. All the other higher value PII fields will not be accessible. This would be sufficient to perform an identity check on the customer in question, but not enough to see anything super sensitive in the one view.

---

[11] This is a lot easier to do now thanks to services like the Google Authenticator App.

Now it could be that the Customer Care Role also needs to go in and see more sensitive information (say tax details) if this were the case the Role of the Customer Care rep would become temporarily privileged to have specific access for the customer in question. In effect new lower & upper PII value bounds come into effect for the duration of the increase in privilege.

Although, given the need to implement a way for Data Subjects to see their PII, the Data Subject could use the same mechanism to see the sensitive information directly? Decisions like this come down to the complexities involved and what's manipulated. But if the overhandling of sensitive information reduces, a PII leak risk goes, down and the operational costs reduce as well.

Monitoring and Alerting

All this limit setting and controls are great, but they need backing up with a suitable level of oversight and escalation. The oversight can both be passive and active as follows:

- **Last logged and last activity tracking** – when a user logs in show them the time they previously logged in and when they were last active. Most people have routines and a good knowledge of when they last did something, so this will instantly highlight account misuse. This should be straightforward to implement as the information should already be in the user record for logging purposes.
- **Group activity** – If you have a group of users fulfilling a role (say customer care). Provide somewhere in the UI a list of who is currently active. This way the group provides oversight and for instance, would notice if Fred's account was active while they were on holiday.
- **Alert Button** – If the user spots something wrong, they need a straightforward way of alerting management and security, provide a simple button and form that captures the required info and raises a ticket as needed.

By putting such evident monitoring in at a group level, two things are achieved:

1. It guarantees many eyes are available to see if there is anything amiss, and,
2. It's very evident to a potentially bad actor or hacker that such monitoring is occurring, which they know increases the likelihood of capture, so reducing their reward.

Concerning escalation, it's something best done programmatically, expecting people to perform an escalation process manually is expecting far too much. Plus, it usually makes a single person responsible for running the process, where escalation is concerned there should be no critical individuals to its operation.

Hence why we previously mentioned ticketing, this isn't something that should operate solely via email, a structured ticketing system must be used[12]. The same system should also be used for generic security escalations, and the process should be uniform and documented.

Security Information and Event Management

If there are more extensive security requirements (say across multiple systems and services), it could be well worth it to invest in setting up a SIEM (Security Information and Event Management) framework. This combines Security Information Management (SIM) and Security Event Management (SEM) services to give real-time analysis of security alerts generated by multiple applications and networking infrastructure. Such a system works by harvesting events from all contributing systems, aggregating and correlating the events, then deciding if alerts need to be generated. All this information is usually accessed through a universal dashboard with built-in forensic analysis functions.

---

[12] Many cloud-based help-desks and ticket support systems are now available, costing $5 up to $200 per agent per month depending on feature set required.

In such a situation it could be well worth it to extend the range of events generated to include:

- The viewing and editing of PII;
- Account modifications (password changes and role changes in particular).

Setting up a SIEM needs not be expensive, there are open source[13] solutions available.

Alert Fatigue

Something to be careful of when setting up a SIEM and feeding all your data points into it is something known as Alert Fatigue – this is where so many alerts get generated operators become desensitized in their ability to work out what is a genuine alert from a false alarm. This is where proper categorisation of the alerts based on their veracity and automatic escalation occurs, so removing the SIEM operator as the critical link in the response process.

Ideally, implement logic prior to your SIEM that allows cross-correlation on certain key alerts to then produce a 'meta alert' for proven alarm conditions. This should be straightforward if following the PII store model, as there will be a 'quiet zone' inside to work with.

Insider Threat Detection

Insider threat detection is part of UEBA (User & Entity Behaviour Analysis). The UEBA system uses a wide range of information sources (from the SIEM, file accesses, role information, HR records, etc). The distinction between the UEBA and SIEM is that the SIEM is providing coverage of the whole threat landscape, whereas the UEBA is purely internal activity focussed.

Insider threat detection can also depend upon other employees noticing odd or inconsistent behaviour and there being a process in place to report such activity.

---

[13] https://siemonster.com/

Encryption at Rest

An important topic to cover is how exactly the business is to implement encrypting your PII at rest. A typical solution, especially for those on cloud frameworks, is to utilise underlying low-level encryption of the storage medium itself, so instead of encrypting a single file or directory – encrypt the whole disc or a partition on the disc. Then the PII which requires protection goes onto the encrypted medium, usually as part of some database type service.

On the face of it, this solves the issue of the hardware theft and PII being revealed. In its simple case, it has, but such low-level encryption will not protect the information at an application level. Take the system set up shown below.

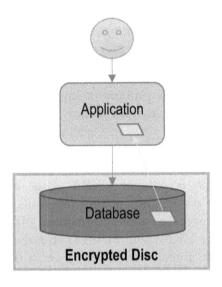

At the bottom is a database holding PII (the yellow parallelogram) which runs on an encrypted disc. An application processing the PII then accesses the database, so reading PII from the database unencrypted.

So, what happens if a hacker attacks the application or if there is a bug which reveals the PII the application is processing? Yes, the PII gets out, and the encryption used on the disc provides no protection from this sort of attack once PII goes to another system to utilise.

The above design pattern occurs in simple usage cases, say a website in which all the code that talks to the database and constructs queries are contained within the website code. Website frameworks that utilise this style of database access include WordPress, Drupal, Magento, and integrated frameworks that do not enforce a strong separation of concerns between front-end code and database access and query manipulation[14].

Now even if there is a more mature system architecture, which wraps the database via an API by which all access goes, there are still some problems, see the diagram below.

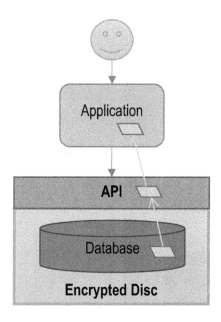

In this system, the application no longer talks directly to the database; it has no code to construct or manipulate database queries (which is a very good thing). Yet now both the API and the Application 'see' plain PII. So,

---

[14] The risk here is an attacker only needs to compromise the web site server to get unfettered access to the backend database, as all the credentials and connections are there to utilise.

a hacker or a bug could still reveal PII. So how does one you get around this?

The trick is to see that, much of the time, PII is:

- Along for the ride,
- Not processed as such, just manipulated as an entity.

This means PII often consists of strings of characters (like a name, address, tax file number, etc.) or a block of data (person's image) that's not processed itself, instead its handed around between systems until it's usually displayed in some form (be that on screen or printed). No one adds up Names or multiplies people's images; they're transferred from one system to the next.

So, given this why not encrypt such PII itself right until we need to display it? See the diagram below.

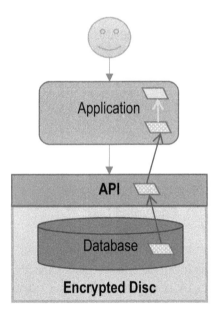

The PII at rest is encrypted in of itself (coloured green), and it's not until it gets to the application that a function is called to perform the decryption.

This has the following attractive qualities:

- Access to the database itself will not reveal PII; you need the decryption key(s) to get to the original PII.
- Developers of the API never 'see' plain PII, they just pass it around. So, reducing the development exposure footprint to PII.
- Database administrators are similarly unable to do anything with the encrypted PII.
- The encryption of the PII provides direct control over who can utilise it, no more sneaky dumping or processing from the database directly; it must go through official channels.
- A hacker not only has to attack the application successfully, but they also need to get access to the mechanism or function which provides the decryption service.
- Freedom in defining the mechanism used for determining the encryption, either symmetric or asymmetric[15] keying either with single keying across a whole table or individual keying per record. All comes down to the value of the PII kept and therefore the effort required to then secure.

Yes, the keys require management, and there will be a very slight hit on performance, but this a small price to pay for reducing the security surface and removing some risk vectors. See the earlier coverage of key management in PII at Rest in Chapter 9 for more details.

In a way, this is internalising the Zero Trust Networking model into the data flow itself; by design, there is no trusting of any system in the data flow chain.

If there are concerns about the storage keys usage at the edge of the service; at the API, the PII can be decrypted and then encrypted using an 'edge' key. Such a key could be distinct to each edge service as required. Again, there is a slight performance hit, but this will decouple the mechanisms used to secure the PII at rest from its final usage.

---

[15] Useful if you want precise control over who can write PII to store.

What about indexing?

Searching across the PII can be a requirement, for instance looking someone up by their name or date of birth. So how to reconcile encrypting the PII and indexing it?

If only supporting exact lookups, merely hash index the fields cared about, i.e. make a copy of the field that contains the hash of unencrypted content (with an algorithmically determined salt). The assumption here is that the likelihood of a clash on the hashes is so low as to not be of concern (even if there is a clash, its resolved higher up by filtering on the actual PII value returned).

If ranged or imprecise lookups are required, either use Anonymisation techniques to create indexes or enumerate the range and turn it into a series of direct lookups (do put limits on the range allowed).

Another option is to change the business workflows not to require searching the records via their PII fields.

Financial Information

Financial Account transactions over time are what typically form financial information. Such transactions are for a set amount of money between two parties at a given moment in time. On the face of it, this all seems to be PII, but it's only so because of the ease of establishing the parties involved. If we structure the data, so the identities of the involved parties are at 'arm's length' to the transactions themselves, then the ability to map the transaction itself back to the individuals involved is more difficult.

The easiest way to achieve this separation is to:

- Store the transactions in one database or data store, with no other information (such as account numbers, tokens, etc.).
- Store the information on the individuals in another distinct database or data store (with distinct access controls, no shared accounts)

- Either use a foreign key or a hash[16] (better) to link the individuals to the transaction records as needed.

With such a set-up, if the transactional store is compromised, no PII about the individuals involved is revealed, it's just a lot of anonymous transactions between unknown parties. This still means mathematical operations can occur on the transactions and selections made, so the manipulation of the transactions isn't compromised, just a little more complicated to enact.

Interestingly, such anonymous transactions are now not PII, as they are unusable on their own and cannot combine with publicly available data sets to re-discover the individuals. A proper degree of security control still needs applying though (mostly around access control and ensuring integrity), they are just not in the same 'class' as regular PII.

To preserve separation, it's critical that if the data sets merge, say to produce statements, that such merged data is:

- Temporal in nature, once used it's deleted completely,
- If it's stored, it can only be on an encrypted medium, distinct to any encryption keys used.

Important Note#1: The assumption here is that the transaction does not contain any other information, for instance, a comment, coding or note. If it does, then it could be PII if that additional information allows the discovery of an individual.

Important Note#2: It's highly likely other regulations will be in play concerning operating financial services and money laundering prevention; which may require additional security and operational controls.

---

[16] GUID's or even a many to one hash, so multiple transactions involving the same party look different until resolving the hash.

Holding PII for Others

When operating a business providing a software service into which customers are entering the PII of their customers in turn, requires preservation of the chain of responsibility as concerns regulations. Such a situation comes about providing Software as a Service (SaaS).

The business needs to 'step up' to the problem in hand and enforce security controls as if it was their own customer PII, i.e. everything previously mentioned applies but it's done in a way that the customers enact the policies and procedures through the business. In the end, there are two pools of PII to deal with:

- Business own owned and operated PII – say on the customers;
- The PII hosted for the customers.

The trick is that these two types of PII cannot co-exist in the same system. Otherwise, there is a risk of a lateral attack compromising the whole customer base across what's a different regulatory domain. Avoid this at all costs, as such an attack will end the SaaS business.

Another factor to be aware of is that the SaaS business might not know what PII is within their systems. For the sake of argument, the business could provide a highly configurable cloud-based HR system; one customer might be storing basic name, holiday and contact details in it; another might also be storing salary, tax, and medical details as well. In this case, any datums or fields which *could* hold PII need treating as if they *are* holding PII and appropriately secured (encryption at rest, encrypted transports, and access controls, etc.).

Something else to guard against is the PII or data of one customer seen or manipulated by another customer. This risk often lies dormant in cloud systems that federate all their customer data together into a big database and use some customer ID or primary key to 'pick out' only the records that concern that customer at that moment in time. If that picking mechanism should ever fail or become compromised, a hacker can walk at leisure through the database for *all* customers.

Another thing to watch out for is hosting customers on different Quality of Service or SLA levels on the same shared infrastructure. This rarely works out as intended, as everybody is in the same bucket regardless of what he or she have paid for or expects. The downside is that someone on the free level could act in a way that either compromises the security of the whole, or they trigger a bug that 'bricks' the whole infrastructure. Even pushing out a new feature is risky, as there is no mechanism to roll out layer by layer, starting with those who paid the least. With no actual separation between the SLA levels, crosstalk is possible (if not inevitable) which could lead to a chain reaction bringing everything to a halt. Do this right from the start and separate via SLA level, everyone will sleep easier.

Legal Agreements

The SaaS business needs to get its customers to sign an agreement with them that if they hold PII with the business that they uphold their obligations with respect to the regulations as well. This could mean:

- They need to appoint a Data Controller;
- Have in place Data Subject Access procedures;
- Mechanisms of contact and representation for regulatory authorities to use;
- Appropriate security controls and documentation to show enactment;
- Reporting and recording of PII Usage;
- Mechanisms for PII sharing and anonymisation.

It could be some of this the SaaS business provides as a service, but the onus is with customers to use as intended, hence why they need to sign an agreement to prove they have understood this. This way if their proven wanting, it's the customer's willful act of noncompliance which is the core issue.

To further complicate things, this agreement needs to cover off:

- **Rebranded product offerings and resale** – in effect the PII isn't the business's customers, it's their customers.
- **International regulations** – the customers business location and where their customers are needs consideration to determine which regulations need covering off. The business might even need to

restrict itself to individual countries and forego business in certain difficult countries.

Also remember, that unless the business is running its own cloud service from top to bottom, they are in turn are holding PII on someone else's infrastructure. It's more than likely they will have already come across updated terms and conditions and requirements placed upon the business by the cloud hosting provider already.

Given all the above, it's critical a SaaS business gets good legal & security advice and errs on the side of caution.

As previously discussed, start-ups that offer SaaS products on the cloud need to be especially careful; if their product suddenly takes off, they can go overnight from having minimal PII compliance requirements to having maximal PII compliance because of their sudden jump in operational and financial size. At the very least such start-ups need to ensure they have the right systematic foundations in place (encryption, logging, and access control) to quickly set up on top all the procedures and services required. They should also be careful not to underestimate the cost and effort of such an undertaking. Their scaling up could also require other regulations to be complied with at the same time.

Training

For the change in how to treat PII to be effective, it's essential that personnel all understand the reasons why and get training in how to protect and preserve security.

At the very least everyone is aware of:

- What regulations, at a high level, the business is required to comply with and what the punishments are for noncompliance.
- What the procedures are, especially around:
  - o Hiring and vetting (background checks and references);
  - o Access Permissions and Role assignment;
  - o Data Subject Access requests;

    - 3rd Party Access;
    - Incident Response and Escalation,
    - Visitor signing in and out.
- Specific Operational Risks:
    - Social Engineering – independently verify, do not assume trust.
    - Office Security Controls – keeping doors locked, visitors always escorted, alarms, tailgating, etc.
    - Machine Security – laptops encrypted, screen saver timeouts, etc.

The training is organised to confirm and log understanding. New hires must undergo training *prior* to accessing the live PII.

Application Considerations

When accessing or manipulating PII in an application, there are few things to keep in mind.

1. All access to PII must be across a secure transport (say HTTPS).
2. Only display the minimal amount of PII at a time to allow people to do their job. For instance, not permitted is a screen that lists people's names and addresses wholesale.
3. By default, do not permit people to 'dump' records. PII should not be extractable from the application.
4. Implement strict inactivity timeouts on screens that display PII. This way if someone walks away from the app it should quickly go back to a none PII containing screen OR a mask is displayed over the screen requiring authentication to remove.
5. For sensitive fields do not just display, use a 'show' button as a confirmative action (that's logged as an event) to see the field contents.
6. The application must not store locally any working data which could contain PII. For web-based applications, this means disabling caching entirely on PII containing screens. Disable caching for REST APIs.

7. Implement the ability to invalidate user sessions centrally, so if an account's compromised, prevent all access using that account. In effect, keep a per-user revision field in the user record and session and frequently check to be the same. If different void the session.
8. Application runtime logging must always mask out any PII, regardless of whether it's regular logging or debug logging. The masking can be turned off by a specific positive configuration control (by default it's on), but that must become a manual action in the production environment. Have tests during the release process to ensure the masking is working.

Application Security

Apart from the above, application security principals apply, including:

- Code scanning both automated and manual,
- Defensive programming techniques,
- Functional and non-functional security scans,
- Pen testing
- Vulnerability tracking and remediation.

The application development process needs implementing in such a way that no one tool or method is responsible for providing coverage alone at *any* step of the process. A security specialist needs to be able to step in and spot check as required based on experience, a blind trust in tools is fatal, as they can only discover what they're coded to find (which is always behind the times and does not exactly match all usage situations). Consider this implementing Defence in Depth in the application development process.

Remember, most external attacks succeed either based on software vulnerabilities or web application failures (SQL injection, cross-site scripting, remote file inclusion, etc.). The application is often the first line of defence and deserves due care and attention.

REST API's

It is common now for systems to make use of REST API's either at the externally visible system edge or to implement some internal service. There are some special security considerations that need to be taken into account.

1. Never run a REST API on port 80. This may seem counterinitiative, but if run on port 80 it makes it harder to control basic access and implement effective usage monitoring at a network level (say by an IDS). Also, by running on port 80, the risk is run of a bad firewall rule assumption (Ops, it must be a public website) opening up an internal API to the world at large.
2. All parameters are checked for what they are and NOT what they are not. Bad parameters must result in an error event log.
3. Perform all SQL injection, XSS screening, etc in the API, as you do not know in advance if the API will be integrated with a web-facing service which does not implement such checks. Never assume the calling service will do this.
4. Insist the means of authentication for the calling service detail whom the call is being made on behalf of (i.e. system ABC calling for user Fred). This way a useful log trail is made.
5. Never have an API perform public and internal client services off the same instance, this creates a risk of an external DDoS killing all access. Also means the public API could enact internally privileged actions. Keep what serves the public and what is internal well apart.
6. Never suffer internal REST API's being trivially publicly tunnelled., i.e. via a simple proxy. See the previous point for why not.

Advanced Masking

An alternative approach to masking (given that it needs to be done both at the front end and with any logging) is to use a controlling attribute of how to display fields containing PII.

This all hinges on the Front End using software patterns like MVC (Model View Controller), PAC (Presentation Abstraction Control) or ADR (Action Domain Responder) with a strong field display abstraction around the objects displayed. In other words, rather than 'naked' fields given to the Template or View, there is a specific Rendering service that knows for each type of field what to render in the given display context, which saves rewriting the same formatting code for each instance of a given field type and ensure consistency (it also helps with internationalisation).

The 'trick' here is to:

1. Extend the Field type attributes to show if they contain PII or not.
2. Extend the Rendering service to accept a '*doMasking*' flag.
3. Modify the per type rendering services to perform masking if the *doMasking* flag is set.
4. Utilise the *doMasking* flag in the display context.
5. Insist all logging of object fields must go through a rendering service with the *doMasking* flag set unless overridden explicitly in the application configs.

Another alternative is to have the logging service automatically mask anything between a predetermined pair of delimiting characters, say '[[' and ']]' unless the override is set in the application configs.

Chapter 12
The PII Vault

We are losing privacy at an alarming rate – we have none left.

John McAfee

As mentioned before, it's quite common, once looking for it, for PII to show up all over the place. When acting on securing PII there a few choices:

- Focus on the high-value PII and ignore the low-value PII
- Secure everything that has PII
- Extract the PII and hold it in one very secure system

The first option isn't viable as well-known even low-value PII when combined with other information can lead to massive privacy problems and the identification of individuals wholesale. It's not likely to achieve regulatory compliance going down this route.

The second option, unless the business has only one or two systems, can be costly and provides no actual guarantee of success, as there is an extensive security surface to keep secure always. Those systems all still need to do their day jobs as well; best of luck!

This leaves just the third option, explored here.

The definition of PII Vault is:

A dedicated system charged with the secure storage and manipulation of PII within a business that helps it meet its core regulatory requirements.

Such a vault provides an API to other systems & services in the business to access the PII, and there is <u>no other approved method</u> by which the PII is accessed or stored. This is a critical feature as it's enforcing a standard

231

'gateway' to the PII through which all systems must pass. This makes it possible to implement:

- Fine grain control over which systems can access and manipulate which PII.
- Log which systems access which PII.
- Monitoring of usage patterns and detection of unusual patterns of access;
- Notification of systems when some PII changes.
- Monitoring PII freshness and correctness.
- Automatic deletion of PII when no longer used.
- Generation of data owner reports.
- Centralised anonymisation functions.
- Strong encryption and secure key management.
- Multisite deployments for reliability.
- Finely tuned security monitoring.
- Data standards and consistency.

Imagine trying to implement that list of requirements across multiple existing systems, and you will instantly see why the PII Vault concept has so much going for it. It's that much easier to codify and enforce various PII policies from a central location.

Also, by implementing such a stand-alone system its services and features are tested and proven independently of the systems which will depend upon it. This should be easier and quicker to achieve than trying to 'shoehorn' such testing & development consistently into existing systems.

Plus, for the systems that need to talk to the PII Vault, they only need to change how they access and manipulate PII to go via the vault, assuming a certain degree of separation of concerns and architecture design in the systems in question.

Further, due to the removal of PII from their systems, it could help rationalise their technology usage (they may no longer have a need for a database or a search service). They might even be able to reduce their security requirements depending on what information remains in the system. It could also improve their performance as well.

There is also the possibility that the functional footprint of what remains of a system is so small that merging such functionality into other systems is better for operational cost reasons.

Now some of you may say this is putting all your PII eggs in the one basket, and that is true, but this basket is secure, scalable, reliable and provably so in a regulatory sense. Should all the systems to be still carrying such a heavy responsibility or is better for just the PII Vault to carry it?

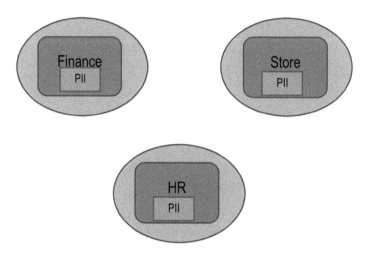

To put this into a visual form, consider having the following systems:

Each of the three systems holds PII, but this PII also means there is a PII breach risk per system, which then means implementing security controls per system to keep that PII safe, assuming not using the Zero Trust Networking model, shown by the oval around each system. This is a significant surface to monitor and ensure is suitably secure.

Now compare this to the situation where there is a PII vault.

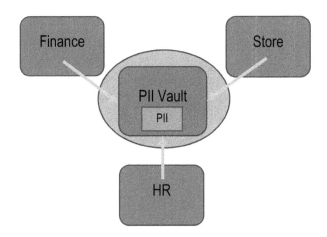

The PII has been migrated to the PII Vault, so anyone accessing the other systems will have to get through those systems then try to get into the PII Vault to get their hands on the PII. Now all the PII is in one place it's much easier to ensure it remains secure as there is only the one system to worry about from a pure PII perspective.

It's important to remember that the other non-PII holding systems still need proper security controls, it just that taken away from them is the risk of a PII breach at scale.

When a PII Vault is Needed

So, given the PII value, when should a business consider this option? If from the PII Analysis done, there is:

- Sensitive PII (SPII) in <u>any</u> system, or,
- A single table score over 100, or,
- An aggregate system scores over 100, or,
- Aggregate all systems score over 150

Strongly consider the PII Vault solution because the PII has high intrinsic worth to cybercriminals and the public and has sufficient total volume to make it worth obtaining. Also, any system scoring over 150 indicates information that's not trusted to a third party to look after (in that the business completely outsources it and has no direct control over the implementation), the breach risk is something that needs direct management in-house (with staff and contractors in your employ) to be 100% sure.

Such a vault can also form an integral part of the Personal Information Management System (PIMS) strategy, as it's much easier to write up and enact a PIMS framework when the PII is centralised. Also, the regulatory environment the business operates in could well require the usage of a PIMS with appropriate security controls (GDPR being an example), so why not take the opportunity to make life easier and centralise the PII.

Also, consider if there is SPII, that may need to go into its own standalone vault to comply with the regulations – it could be possible to implement both PII and SPII Vaults off the same code base.

It's also important to remember that you will need to deal with Data Subject Access Requests and maintain data processing records (see the previous chapter); although these systems can be considered 'privileged clients' for the respective Vaults.

Key-Value Stores and Databases

It's crucial that the vault does not become a data 'dumping ground', it should only hold PII and nothing else and be ruthlessly strict about this as it will directly impact the ability to assure security. In particular, do not make the vault also perform any Authentication or Authorisation service for any other system, this is best done by its own dedicated system, so thereby reducing the risk of password breaches and enabling the introduction of additional security controls with ease (login behaviour monitoring across services and 2FA).

Although given this if there are many contributing systems there could be quite a set of fields to deal with, and this number of fields will not go down over time, quite the opposite.

To avoid the nightmare of having to keep tweaking schemas every other week, consider using key-value store solutions (or adding in support for that into the database, later). The benefit here is the storage of additional fields just becomes another key in a record in the store, no need to be tweak schemas. Although required is control over:

- What are the accepted keys,
- What are the accepted values and formats of the value per key
- Which systems see what keys and in turn write or read to/from them.

Which the schema approach does anyway, so should be little additional cost to implement.

It's possible to combine the database and key-value store approaches in three ways:

- Dedicated database with a dedicated key-value store;
- Dedicated database with a key-value store table;
- Dedicated database with a key-value store column.

Each of these has its own pros and cons as follows:

- The use of a dedicate key-value store creates a synchronisation and atomic transaction problem, in that a creation of a record in the database needs to include the committing of the changes to the key-value store as well, depending on which key-value store system is used, this could be expensive to confirm and take considerable system time.
- The use of a key-value table within the database gives the transactional behaviour but be careful of creating a many table locking behaviour that could impact performance (need row-level locking). The advantage of this is if the keys and the foreign keys are indexed correctly, there is a natural 'do you have' lookup system in place – which could prove useful for data selection.
- The use of a key-value column gives a quick, space efficient and straightforward way to store key-value pairs (say JSON encoded), but there is limited ability to inspect efficiently key distribution and the values (unless the database supports indexing JSON fields as a type). Also, if storing many pairs this way the cost to recover just one can become expensive at the limit. This is another good reason for the PII Vault not to become a dumping ground.

The usual deciders if a given field goes into a key-value store often depends if it's extensively used as an indexed lookup field or if the value is often read from or written to.

Deployment Model

The goal here is to adopt Defence in Depth techniques to protect the PII logically and physically and that the depth of defence is proportional to the value of the PII kept in the vault. Remember the security needs to be provable by design.

There are few implementation options available; explained below with the expected minimal security requirements for each.

Public Cloud Deployment

This is where public cloud providers (such as Amazon, Google or Microsoft) host the PII Vault for you. In this case, the PII Vault is set up as follows:

- Put under its own distinct administrative group, in effect admins need to log into a specific account to administrator the deployment;
- Administrative and privileged accounts all implement MFA.
- Put under its own distinct network segment or group;
- Use a whitelist network access control list, not permitted is universal access out to the internet (it's allowed by default, be careful). Although to allow updates access out to the update servers for the OS used will need permitting.
- API Access via a whitelist of servers under business control.
- The API is never made visible via proxy or middleware forwarding 'as is' to servers not under business control (i.e. not visible from the Internet).
- API operates an encrypted transport.
- Storage encrypts at rest.
- Admin access to machines via a restricted bastion service.

How to implement is a matter of choice, although using the Zero Trust Networking model, consider operating the vault in its own distinct Control Plane to remove the risk of a shared Control Plane compromise impacting the PII security.

The cloud provider also needs to provide certification that they maintain suitable physical access controls to their hosting environment (ISO27001 compliance ideally). A good sign they do this is if they are PCI DSS compliant. In fact, if they are PCI DSS compliant they may have a cloud deployment template ready to go that will meet the requirements with a few tweaks.

Private Cloud Deployment

This is where the business operates its own cloud deployment framework, all the conditions for the public cloud deployment apply, plus:

- The physical rack on which the PII Vault service resides needs distinct locking (a key or combination lock only for that specific rack that is kept in a secure place distinct to the other rack keys) and be under continuous recording CCTV observation both front and back.
- Log physical access to the rack and sign it off. Sign in and out the keys specifically.

The assumption here is the private cloud instance is already in a secured colocation environment.

Dedicated Machines

If implementing the PII Vault directly on machines (either dedicated or a cloud environment, which the business owns and operates, in effect a Private Cloud) then do the following in addition to all the conditions above.

- The machines must be in a secured room environment[1] with a single hardened door that always locks and requires a key or code

---

[1] All modes of access require some key or code (for instance the windows must be lockable).

to open. That door must be under constant CCTV surveillance from the insecure side (facing towards the path of entry, so it captures faces) at least for movement detection recording.

- The door lock must not trigger open by movement from the secure side[2], use either a handle or button to unlock.
- The room itself must be part of the building or floor alarm environment with a PIR sensor.
- The machines must mount in a rack, and that rack bolts to a solid surface in a way that prevents removal without access to the inside of the rack.
- In the rack must be shelves above and below the machines to prevent access through the top or bottom of the rack.
- The front and back of rack must both lock, the sides cannot remove without a key. The front and back of the rack cannot be glass; they must be either solid steel or meshed steel. Do make sure the key isn't a generic shared key, if required get in a locksmith to ensure the keys are unique.

If using a physical key, maintain a key sign-out & sign-in register. If using a pin code lock, either every 6 months or when someone who knows the pin leaves, change the pin to a previously unused code.

Alternatively, the machines can go into a dedicated vault room or cage within the colocation operation[3]. The key qualities of such a caged room are:

- Steel meshed grid on all sides including into the ceiling void and below the raised floor (close off the crawl spaces, no popping tiles to get in).
- The entrance door is key locked or uses a PIN code lock. Shroud the internal exit button or switch to prevent activation by prodding through the mesh.
- Constantly recording CCTV inside.
- The door itself must resist brute force opening.

---

[2] If using a PIR sensor an air conditioner breeze could cause the door to unlock on its own, which has been known to occur.
[3] https://en.wikipedia.org/wiki/Colocation_centre

Now, this may seem dramatic but is based on the experience that the physical security of equipment is as important as the software and network security. The more controlled the physical access, the less likely an accidental or intentional physically based breach.

Never allowed

Below is a list of things never allowed as part of the Vault physical implementation:

- Devices with wireless network functionality (such as Bluetooth or Wi-Fi). No wireless network cards allowed.
- Disable access to USB ports at the OS level, disconnected inside or physically blocked.

Now, some may consider this 'overkill' but remember the business needs to be able to prove it has sufficient security around the PII. Ad hoc mechanisms with no documentation trail are not adequate; security needs to be 'designed in' and evident.

BCM Requirements

Also remember, for BCM reasons, there is either a secured off-site storage facility or if minimising downtime a hot-hot copy (duplicate set up with a mirrored data set) that is ready to go live as needed. Also, guard against single points of failure in the system design, perhaps using the N+1 redundancy technique.

> A single point of failure is a single instance of a critical system, component or service that needs to be up 24x7 without fail for services to work. If it fails on its own, everything goes down.

Such mirroring can either be a function of the high-level application, something provided by the data storage system or an aspect of the virtualisation service in use. The key point is that it's considered to be extremely reliable in operation.

> The N+1 technique is when at least N+1 servers are available when only N are needed to deal with the load. This way if one fails everything keeps going. Autoscaling on the cloud achieves the same goal using dynamic resource capacity assignment.

Software Implementation

The software environment or framework chosen to implement the Vault code must have the following qualities:

- Can examine <u>all</u> code. Such as contributing libraries and frameworks.
- Supported with a vulnerability notification process (sign up to a mailing list to get security updates).
- Well supported and well known by engineers.
- Works well with release management tools.

As the code develops, it's stored in a code repository service with strong access controls and must be private always.

Regardless of the development methodology or process undertaken (Agile, Waterfall, etc.) incorporate into the build process automatic code scanning[4] at the unit level (so security problems map directly to a developer team) and perform automated penetration testing[5] against a test instance. Note: This is not a substitute for manual scanning, it acts as a backstop to stop common security mistakes getting into production.

---

[4] https://www.owasp.org/index.php/Source_Code_Analysis_Tools
[5] https://www.owasp.org/index.php/Testing_Guide_Introduction#Penetration_Testing

Personal Information Security & Systems Architecture

During implementation aim for a system structure like that shown below.

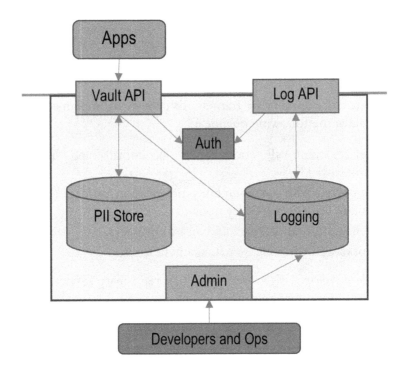

There a few key considerations to take onboard here:

- Perform system authentication and authorisation within the vault against a whitelist; i.e. specific system accounts need to be on a list and have the right calling credentials as well.
- Assume user authentication and authorisation occurred prior, although the API still needs to know the user account information to go into the logs. If required, the calling system can pass along role information, and we can whitelist the roles against permitted actions. This can be a fiddle to implement but is a useful safeguard.
- The apps can only see the Vault and Log API.
- Store logs distinct to the PII store. Permitting locking down of log access, log signing and indexing to support auditing activity.

- Implement the Log API distinctly to the main Vault API, reducing the risk of a horizontal attack[6] and less code churn[7] for the Log API. No log alteration permitted by the Log API (also use a database account specifically restricted to read-only access on the log).
- Use of the admin backend results in a logged event.
- Access to the admin backend is only possible from a set of machines distinct from those used by the apps, ideally in a completely different security zone.
- Failures in authentication or authorisation **MUST** be logged and generate an alert. Similarly, log failures to correctly enact the API (i.e. 404's, missing parameters or badly formed values; if not PII sensitive record the whole request).
- Everything that comes in via the API <u>must</u> be tested for what it should be, <u>not</u> for what it isn't. e.g. if you expect an integer type, test for the presence of an integer (+/- and digits) not for if it contains alphabetic characters etc[8]. If you expect just a string containing a word, test for only A to Z, etc. This even applies to compound data types (e.g. JSON, XML, etc.).
- Everything that comes in via the API must be range checked by value and length. So, if you expect a string with a maximum of 20 characters, reject anything over 20 characters. This acts as an additional safeguard against buffer overflows, and arithmetic overflows.

If the business has implemented PCI DSS, most of this will be familiar.

Remember all access to the PII needs logging, as the business needs to be able to respond to external requests to detail PII usage, so logged is:

- When the access occurred,

---

[6] A hacker jumping laterally through a system into another function.

[7] The rate of changes in the code and how often new releases result.

[8] In effect you whitelist all parameter values or use Regex (if simple, a provable state machine otherwise). This is a critical mechanism to prevent injection. You might also need to sanitize such values, which is where what's not wanted is stripped (such as removing unwanted HTML), although be careful with this (language theory parsing) and use proven libraries when available.

- What system accessed,
- On behalf of what user account,
- What the action was.

In a way which is tamper proof to anyone with access to the logging service internals. This usually implies record signing and chained signing akin to blockchain to increase the effort required to forge the logs. Keep such logs for a minimum of 6 months, longer if able.

> Chained signing is when the signature of a record depends on the record contents and the signature of the previous record and signing key. In this way modifying or deleting a record requires changing all records that follow it.

Also, record the access to the log for such information in the log itself. Also, ensure that the log never contains any PII.

Dependency Minimisation

A subject rarely touched on with computer systems and architecture design is that of detailed dependency management, namely managing the internal and external dependencies of a system to minimise outages and maintain control of the security surface.

Management of the dependencies for the vault is critical to its success. Too many external dependencies and there is a risk of having to update the system just due to dependency changes, which can be expensive to enact. More worrying is the 'at arm's length' or undocumented changes that do occur from time to time due to a breakdown in communications. Overnight a system can go down with no immediate cause, on examination it's found some remote service has moved or upgraded its operations in a none backwards compatible way.

The rule of thumb here is the bigger the value of the data stored, the more efforts undertaken to minimise external dependencies first, then worry about internal dependencies. Reason being the internal dependencies can be managed in a timely fashion, whereas the external dependencies might require dealing with on short notice. Pay attention to security-related services, the viability of the security of the vault should not ride on an external third party over which the business has little influence. Remember the business may just be one of thousands of customers to them. We also recommend if using such third parties that the dependency be as 'lite' as it can be to make it easy to move to another provider if required, so avoiding using services and features only available from one vendor. **Avoid lock-in at all costs**.

Another mechanism to make appropriate use of when managing external dependencies is to leverage standards. Those associated with protocols and data representation are most helpful. This will make it easier to change to another provider when required. As mentioned above avoid any vendor-specific extensions to standards, this will create a lock-in via proxy.

Technology Alphabet Soup

Be aware of using too many technologies and languages in your implementation. If possible have no more than 2 types of anything in the system (ideally just 1 if possible). So, implementing in Java and Scala is fine, but if using Python as well, the rule brakes.

The reasons for this are several:

1. The more languages and frameworks involved the more expensive and difficult the system is to maintain.
2. It's harder to get and retain a team with the diverse skills required.
3. The rate of updates and external changes required to keep current are higher. With a resultant increase in the risk of things just breaking.
4. The increase in complexity reduces confidence in security coverage.

Combine this technology diversity limit with the management of your dependencies, and you keep a lot of external architectural headaches under control.

Development Cycle

Before taking code into production for the first time, ensure that at least the following has occurred:

- Automatic code scanning for insecure coding practices[9]. Ideally, it's also checked directly by an information security professional.
- Verify the design as implemented is secure by an information security professional.
- Confirm the deployment environment is secure by an information security professional via a white box pen test whose goal is to obtain access to the PII.

Without such checks, there is little confidence that the PII Vault is secure.

> A pen test is an authorized simulated attack on a system to establish if it's secure and find and document any weaknesses.
>
> A white box pen test is where all development information is shared with the pen tester so that hidden security faults can be more easily discovered.

Regarding the information security professional and their background, the ideal person would have:

- Degree or higher qualification in computer science.
- Minimum 7 years direct experience at major businesses dealing with online security issues (namely defensive techniques, responding to system intrusions and remediation).
- Ideally a recognised certification in security from a leading security organisation or leadership skills in cybersecurity.

This is someone with a combined technical and security background who can examine systems in depth and can work equally with engineers and managers.

If engaging a business or consultancy to perform the security services, do ensure that the work done is signed-off by someone with the above background.

---

[9] https://www.owasp.org/index.php/Source_Code_Analysis_Tools

If possible, try to keep an ongoing relationship with the one security professional, they will come to understand the 'quirks' of the systems and the business and help guide them along a more secure development path – as often such individuals have much wider system experience beyond security. Also, consider if they can assist with security training for engineers and general security awareness; remember security is everyone's concern.

Release Management

Your exact process of release management is down to you, but it must have the following characteristics always:

- Be versioned and traceable, in that part of the release details what changed and why. Also, the versioning MUST follow the Major/Minor/Patch convention.
- Make use of appropriate release management automation tools and frameworks, e.g. Docker, Ansible, Jenkins, etc
- Provably able to roll back a release, i.e. as part of the testing pipeline see if you can rollback. This usually means backwards compatibility or specific snapshot/restore or uninstall scripting.
- Ideally employ package signing to ensure what's made for release is what's going to release.

Although given all the above it is critical you have a 'something hit the fan' exception process; unexpected things can occur when you release into production even with the best laid plans – in this case the exceptional process comes into play and a decision needs to making to fast patch forwards or rollback; the only time you can do nothing is when the problem is in a provably unused feature and there are no unacceptable security risks. Remember the whole point of a release is to release something working that benefits the business. After performing the exception recovery action do the cause analysis and modify your development or release process coverage to catch it.

It's important that absolutely no finger pointing occur throughout the process – we all are human, and mistakes do occur (who hasn't had that sinking feeling), use the opportunity to learn and improve the team professionally.

Also consider if the act of release management and exception handling should be completely within the operations team in consultation with the engineers. Senior engineering management should not need to be in loop with respect decision making during the actual release process, it sets the wrong expectations and flies in the face of proper delegated trust.

Penetration Testing

Penetration testing is usually a periodic check perform against a system in production to probe for weaknesses. Although there is nothing to stop you also using freely available penetration test toolkits[10] to build such a check into either the development or release management cycles as an automated step. This has the advantages of catching a vulnerability prior to it getting to production whilst empowering the developer teams to directly 'own' the security quality of what they produce.

Enhancements

To go to town on the PII Vault security, consider:

- **Server level tripwires** – these detect modifications of critical files on the disc[11].
- **Network traffic monitoring** – this detects abnormal traffic on the vault network[12].

These together provide additional assurance that the machines or services are uncompromised.

Also, implement RASP & Camouflaging techniques in the API's to further frustrate any cybercriminals who are trying to find where PII is in a business (see page 150).

Also, if there are data mining or anonymisation usage cases to consider, it could well be worth developing a specific set of methods to aid such exporting of data dumps. This will make it easier to deal with a variety of

---

[10] http://w3af.org/ runs either standalone or from a Docker container.
[11] https://en.wikipedia.org/wiki/Open_Source_Tripwire
[12] Network Intrusion Prevention system (IPS) and Network Intrusion Detection System (IDS) - https://www.snort.org/

use cases. Also look at what the data mining is and if it's viable to perform some of the more valuable mining on the vault directly.

Also, consider if setting up a bug bounty programme[13] would be appropriate. For instance, if the product interacts online directly with the public and holds a lot of sensitive information, a bug bounty programme could be a useful ongoing check for vulnerabilities, consider it a form of proactive cyber insurance that pays back both for you and the white hat community.

Moving PII into a SaaS Solution

An alternative to implementing a PII Vault is to either:

- Take the PII which is requiring the need for a PII Vault and moving it into a specifically secured SaaS provider, or,
- Moving all the PII into a specifically secured SaaS provider.

An example of this might be an in-house HR system that moves to a cloud provider HR service.

There are few points to keep in mind with this:

- Using a cloud service does not absolve the business of being the responsible maintainer of the PII, they still need to ensure its security.
- The information still needs extracting from the systems, sanitizing and back referencing as required.
- What happens if the SaaS provider goes bankrupt or changes their services, so they no longer cover the use case? A secondary provider arrangement should be in place just in case.

Also, there can also be issues around how quickly the business can respond to data access requests, log requests and being able to notify data breaches in the required period.

---

[13] https://www.bugcrowd.com/

Key Points

- The Vault is the only place to store PII.
- All other systems carry references to the PII.
- A PII Vault can be part of an overall PIMS strategy
- Consider using key-value stores to deal with variety more effectively
- The vault can be either set up on a public or private cloud instance or dedicated machines, just ensure strong security, both logical and physical, around the setup.
- Access logging goes into its own store in the vault to prevent modification.
- During development ensure the code's scanned for insecure coding practices.
- Be careful using a SaaS solution as the business is still the responsible party for the PII.

Chapter 13
Future Trends

If we don't act now to safeguard our privacy, we could all become victims of identity theft.

Bill Nelson

The PII, its management and its significance to people changes daily. From the recent revelations concerning Facebook and Cambridge Analytica's data sharing policy to Mark Zuckerberg's full-page apology in several major US and UK Sunday newspapers; PII is top of everybody's mind.

In this light what are the future trends concerning PII? This chapter tries to answer this question and others, although like all forward-looking analysis what does occur could be completely different. The only certainty is that dealing with PII is going to get more complicated over time.

Regulations

Without a doubt, PII regulations are going to become more detailed. Yet certain ground-breaking regulations, like the GDPR in Europe, are untested in a court of law at the time of writing. Although this is in some way mute, if the regulations cannot be enforced in the court of law, they will just be revised until they do.

Jurisdictions are watching the GDPR like a hawk, for the simple reason being if it proves workable, then adopting similar regulations abroad offers a shortcut in determining regulatory breach and hence action. Trip up in Europe then multiple breaches of regulations could descend like a plague of locust on an unfortunate business.

251

In a similar vein, it's highly likely there will be work to unify the regulations if only for the simple reason to reduce the 'gaps' that businesses could use to escape the regulations.

Also, it is extremely likely the per state tightening of privacy, data security and breach notification regulations will continue in the US to fill the regulatory void at the federal level.

Fine Grain Opting-In Everywhere

One area which is undoubtedly due to change is how opting into services occurs. We foresee that regulations will require specific agreement to opt-in to PII sharing with no exceptions. Also forbidden will be the lumping in of the permissions with a Terms and Conditions change, the authorisation to use PII will have to be a distinct agreement, and the presentation of that agreement <u>will</u> be easy to understand. We expect there will be a standardisation of permissions representation to be both visual and written, as well as machine readable privacy policy terms (Chirgwin, 2018).

The regulations will also require in all cases periodic renewing of those permissions, there will no giving of permissions that last forever to businesses and this period of permission will travel with the PII where ever it goes, so third parties will need to keep track of this and delete PII whose rights of usage has expired. This will apply to <u>all</u> PII held by businesses, so if a business does not know when the PII expires, they must either reconfirm permission with the individual in question or delete immediately within a set grace period.

The implementation of the duration of the period of renewal can be by:

- Time since last confirmed interaction with the individual;
- Longer or shorter time periods depending on the sensitivity of the PII in question;
- Maximum time (say 5 years) at which renewal must occur.

The practical upshot of this is the ability of businesses to keep long-term records of people's activities, and attributes in fine detail will be extremely curtailed. Also remember this expiry does not apply to anonymised information, which a business can keep forever if they guarantee it can never reverse to reveal the individual.

Strong Identity & Anonymization

It looks that who is the ultimate holder of the 'base' of a PII record will become a government-approved independent agency. The current 'wild west' of businesses holding distinct records of PII on individuals with no easy ability to see where information has gone will end. This also means existing businesses will have to bring their systems into scope with the 'base key' held by the independent agency on an individual's behalf.

Of course, the 'base key' design is so that no two businesses get the same key for the same individual, so PII cannot be sneakily merged.

The reason for independent agencies is that no one will trust a government-owned entity to not give in to the temptation to snoop into people's activities and information. Plus, the agency cannot make a profit out of the information it holds. The GDPR considers such agencies as a form of a Personal Information Management System (PIMS).

With such an agency it's foreseen that people will be able to decide to either allow 'live' access to their PII or snapshot access, depending on the usage case of the business. For instance, an online store business that just wants to know a name, telephone number and home address would use a snapshotted view; whereas a taxi business could be given live access to ensure they have the up to date contact information.

A more secure alternative might be that a business gets a PII token instead, which they can exchange for specific views into PII based on their credentials and use case. For instance, an online store does not really need to know where someone lives; it just needs to know how much it costs to ship goods. For the online store, they could give that token to a shipping company who does has access to the address, they could give a shipping quote and later enact as needed. That token might also have restrictions associated with it as to what companies can use it, so it cannot be 'sold on'.

This also raises the interesting point that businesses might no longer need to hold PII in detail anymore, in effect the agencies become massive PII Vaults for whole populations. This could be quite cost-effective to businesses as they might not need all the infrastructure previously required, they just hold references to PII. Plus, it also removes most of the compliance risks for a business, as they won't hold directly any PII to lose.

We also foresee that more structured mechanisms of becoming and staying anonymous online will become the norm; in that as awareness increases to the implications of PII sharing, fewer people will wish to do so and hence be proactive in guarding against this.

Note: regarding privacy and the PII vault agencies, currently we have the situation where cybercriminals are collating vast vaults of PII for nefarious reasons. Improving PII security at the limit requires better-distributed anonymity to devalue the information held elsewhere. Yes, there is the Big Brother problem with the agencies, but this exists now and will not be going away any time soon. Also, there is nothing to stop individuals from using multiple agencies in distinct regulatory domains, hence creating distributed anonymity. The precursor to this exists now, with the use of OAuth[1] based authentication services as provided by most major online businesses, the difference is in what's shared out by the central service and the control expressed over that information.

Universal Visibility & Control

One consequence of centralised PII storage is that access control and tracking of PII usage will become universal. Individuals will be able to see the whole picture as concerns the usage of their PII by businesses and take an active role in its management.

---

[1] https://en.wikipedia.org/wiki/OAuth - open standard for access delegation.

Social Networks

With the reduction in businesses ability to hold onto PII and share it with other businesses for profit, the free social networks will have to find alternative ways to generate revenue than just pure advertising. A few social networks will go to the wall for sure, of those left will be those who have found a way to mix in paid for services that add to the social experience for their users. We think this is a good thing as those who use the social networks will become the real customers.

Fine-grain Targeting and Deep Learning

One thing is obvious; individuals have little visibility or knowledge of the vast amount of information currently collected by businesses and how it's used for a whole variety of reasons. Most people are aware that businesses use behavioural tracking to work out marketing tactics, but the amount of information available combined with powerful analytics techniques makes it possible to discover behaviours or factors the individual may not be aware of yet[2]. Add to this the new wave of AI learning algorithms, including Deep Learning, and people analysis can occur in ways hitherto not possible before. Also, as previously mentioned in the Anonymisation Chapter, fine-grain targeting or micro-targeting can lead to privacy breaches, where an advertiser can target an individual.

There is also growing concern that the sheer amount of personal and behavioural information available enables subtle manipulation in terms of what's picked to display on websites or social networks. In effect, it's possible to create a 'content bubble' per individual tuned to their view of the world and how businesses want to target and manipulate that individual.

This 'wild west' approach to targeting individuals will have to come under progressive tighter control to avoid distortion of the news and stop large businesses having effective ownership on how news is: picked, processed

---

[2] https://www.nytimes.com/2012/02/19/magazine/shopping-habits.html

and consumed. Although this certainly will not occur overnight, as people need to take back control over their PII and its dissemination first.

We also suspect that the same selective opt-in rules will apply to tracking.

Blockchain

Blockchain can implement a decentralised trust management framework around PII access management and ownership (Zyskind, Nathan, & Pentland, 2015). Although businesses must avoid the hype of blockchain as it's just an implementation technology, one of many ways of achieving the required qualities. Also, it should not be the sole means of assuring integrity & trust; there should be additional checks and safeguards.

One issue to be aware of is the distributed ledger aspect of blockchain prevents data deletion, is if blockchain is used 'as is' to hold PII, it will fall foul of legislation that requires PII to be deleted (IBM, 2018). Also, there is the question around whom the controllers and processors of the blockchain are in a highly distributed system.

It looks like the nation-state and personal ownership questions and interests across borders will prevent the distributed blockchain solution taking off anytime soon. Then there is the problem that the public does not understand what blockchain is and only associate it with volatile cryptocurrencies, they do not understand how such personal trust relates to just blockchain on its own.

One area certainly worth watching is the intersection of the blockchain, PII and smart contracts. Smart contracts once written and committed to the blockchain cannot change. This creates not only a security challenge (Data61 CSIRO, 2017), in that security issues cannot be later fixed, but a privacy challenge as well. Although, technologies like Zero Knowledge Proofs[3] can assist in implementing privacy while ensuring trust.

---

[3]   https://blog.cryptographyengineering.com/2014/11/27/zero-knowledge-proofs-illustrated-primer/

Private Clouds

Private clouds are going to become more utilised by businesses, not only for the improved security environment they provide; they will also be cost-effective to own and operate. Simple reason being the processing power available at a given cost and power consumption point is still improving, just look at the SOC (System on Chip) integration possible in Smartphones now. You truly have at least one supercomputer in your pocket.

The practical upshot of this miniaturisation is its applied to the cloud hardware frameworks to produce miniature cloud environments 'in a box' that make use of control software like OpenStack[4]. This trend will only continue as having full control of your cloud environment reduces a lot of third-party integration and command & control risks.

Security

With the increased focus on privacy regulations and the obligations that come from that, unifying security will be pivotal in ensuring businesses do not fall foul of regulations. This implies that those businesses which provide SaaS or IaaS services without the required security controls (or depth of security coverage) will be at an immediate operational risk. Those businesses which provide hosting or operational frameworks for websites will need to go the extra mile to ensure security and prevent hijacks.

Security will have to tighten on many open source and commercial frameworks, PII will either require specific treatment or not be in the framework at all (standards need developing for remote PII vault integrations).

This will have a massive impact on denying cybercriminals access to one of the common tools of the trade – namely compromised servers acting as 'drones' in command and control networks. Of course, whether this results in it becoming more expensive for cybercriminals, depends on whether other machine classes (e.g. IoT) undergo a similar increase in

---

[4] https://www.openstack.org/

security hardening. A standard driven mandatory mechanism for commissioning and performing basic securing (password setting and logs collection) across all permanent network devices would be a good start.

Also, to be truly effective, security systems and services will need to be more immediately 'reactive' to attacks. Given the speed at which attacks occur, having a human in the loop for the first response creates a window of opportunity for cybercriminals. This will require better standards driven definition of events, logging, classification and response frameworks to aid tighter integration between various products and hence ensure coverage. Increased usage will occur of AI technologies (such as Deep Learning) to respond quicker to attacks, such technologies are also used with User & Entity Behaviour Analysis (EUBA) to determine abnormal insider activity. Although, to avoid too many false positives (and possible legal issues), incontestable veracity of data sources will be critical.

Businesses will also need to invest more directly in building out an in-house security resource. Bolt-on security, given the increased sophistication of cybercriminals, will no longer be sufficient. Remember regulations, like the GDPR, require security by design throughout systems in a business that manipulate PII. For a lot of businesses, this will require a more intensive focus on improving confidentiality to a level not previously obtained.

References

Anderson, P. R. (2014, Jan 3). *Cambridge's Head of Cryptography: I Would Abolish MI5 - Forbes.* Retrieved from Forbes: https://www.forbes.com/sites/tamlinmagee/2014/01/03/cambri dges-head-of-cryptography-i-would-abolish-mi5/

Apple, IBM chiefs call for more data oversight after Facebook breach. (2018, March 26). Retrieved from Reuters: https://www.reuters.com/article/us-china-forum-data/apple-ibm-chiefs-call-for-more-data-oversight-after-facebook-breach-idUSKBN1H20JU

Chirgwin, R. (2018, May 24). *Doc 'Cluetrain' Searls' privacy engine project is just the ticket for IEEE.* Retrieved from The Register: https://www.theregister.co.uk/2018/05/24/ieee_boards_the_clue train_for_ethics_push/

Data Risk in the Third-Party Ecosystem. (2016, April). *Ponemon Institute© Research Report.*

Data61 CSIRO. (2017, May). Risks and Oppurtunities for Systems using Blockchain and Smart Contracts. Retrieved from https://www.data61.csiro.au/~/media/052789573E9342068C573 5BF604E7824.ashx

Eiji Hayashi, S. D. (2013, July). CASA: Context-Aware Scalable Authentication. *Proceedings of the 9th Symposium On Usable Privacy and Security, SOUPS 2013.* Retrieved from http://cups.cs.cmu.edu/soups/2013/proceedings/a3_Hayashi.pdf

Fellegi-Sunter, & Jaro. (2014). Fellegi-Sunter and Jaro Approach to Record Linkage . In *Memobust Handbook on Methodology of Modern Business Statistics.*

Filiol, E., & Bannier, A. (n.d.). By-design Backdooring of Encryption System - Can We Trust Foreign Encryption Algorithms? . *Black Hat Europe.* 2017.

Gilman, E. B. (2017). *Zero Trust Networks: Building Secure Systems in Untrusted Networks.* doi:ISBN 978-1491962190.

Hoffman, S. (2018, 5 17). *Steve Wozniak tells us: 'We've lost our privacy and it's been abused'.* Retrieved from Business Insider: https://www.businessinsider.com.au/steve-wozniak-weve-lost-our-privacy-and-its-been-abused-2018-5

IBM. (2018, March 19). *Blockchain and GDPR.* Retrieved from IBM: https://www-01.ibm.com/common/ssi/cgi-bin/ssialias?htmlfid=61014461USEN

Javelin Strategy & Research. (2018, February 18). *Identity Fraud Hits All Time High With 16.7 Million U.S. Victims in 2017, According to New Javelin Strategy & Research Study.* Retrieved from Javelin Strategy: https://www.javelinstrategy.com/press-release/identity-fraud-hits-all-time-high-167-million-us-victims-2017-according-new-javelin

Juniper Research. (2015, May 12). *Cybercrime will cost Businesses over $2 Trillion by 2019.* Retrieved from Juniper Research: https://www.juniperresearch.com/press/press-releases/cybercrime-cost-businesses-over-2trillion

Kashyap Thimmaraju, B. S.-P. (2018). Taking Control of SDN-based Cloud Systems via the Data Plane. *Proceedings of the Symposium on SDN Research (SOSR '18).* (p. 15). New York: ACM.

LOUGHRY, J., & UMPHRESS, D. A. (2002, August). Information Leakage from. *ACM Transactions on Information and System Security,* pp. 262-289.

M. Schwartz, P. (2011). The PII Problem: Privacy and a New Concept of Personally Identifiable Information. *86 N.Y.U. L.Q. Rev. 1814.*

Maycotte, H. (2014, Dec 4). *Convince Your Team to Buy In to a Big Data Solution - ASAP.* Retrieved from Forbes: https://www.forbes.com/sites/homaycotte/2014/12/04/convince-your-team-to-buy-in-to-a-big-data-solution-asap/

Michael Barbaro & Tom Zeller, J. (2006, Aug 9). A Face Is Exposed for AOL Searcher No. 4417749. *N.Y. TIMES.*

Ross, A. (2018, May 14). *How cyber threats could grow under GDPR.* Retrieved from Information Age: http://www.information-age.com/cyber-threats-gdpr-123471929/

Shmatikov, A. N. (2008, May 18). Robust De-Anonymization of Large Sparse Datasets. *2008 IEEE Symposium on Security and Privacy*, 111-125. doi:10.1109/SP.2008.33

Singh, S. (1999). *The Code Book.* London: Fourth Estate Ltd.

Stella, S. (2017, December 8). *Public Knowledge Releases Paper Recommending Guiding Principles for Online Privacy Laws.* Retrieved from Public Knowledge: https://www.publicknowledge.org/press-release/public-knowledge-releases-paper-recommending-guiding-principles-for-online-

Vagata, P., & Wilfong, K. (2014, April 11). *Scaling the Facebook data warehouse to 300 PB .* Retrieved from Facebook: https://code.facebook.com/posts/229861827208629/scaling-the-facebook-data-warehouse-to-300-pb/

Yu, E. (2018, May 18). *One in four APAC firms not sure if they suffered security breach.* Retrieved from ZDNet: https://www.zdnet.com/article/one-in-four-apac-firms-not-sure-if-they-suffered-security-breach/

Zyskind, G., Nathan, O., & Pentland, A. (2015). *Decentralizing Privacy: Using Blockchain to Protect.* IEEE.

Abbreviations

2FA	Two Factor Authentication
ADR	Action Domain Responder
BCM	Business Continuity Management
CASB	Cloud Access Security Broker
CIA	Confidentiality, Integrity, and Availability
COTS	Commercial Off the Shelf
CRUD	Create, Read, Update and Delete
CTPH	Context Triggered Piecewise Hashes
DLP	Data Loss Prevention
DPA	Data Protection Act
DPO	Data Protection Officer
DTbD	Data Trust, by Design
ESR	Efficient Security Response
FIPP	Fair Information Practice Principles
FPC	Federal Privacy Commissioner
FTC	Federal Trade Commission
HIPAA	Health Insurance Portability and Accountability Act
HMAC	Hash-based Message Authentication Code
GDPR	General Data Protection Regulation
IaaS	Infrastructure as a Service
IdA	Identity Analytics
IoT	Internet of Things
IDS	Intrusion Detection System
IPS	Intrusion Prevention System
ISMS	Information Security Management System
MFA	Multiple Factor Authentication
MITM	Man in the Middle
MTTF	Mean time to failure
MVC	Model View Controller
NIST	National Institute of Standards and Technology
NPP	National Privacy Principles
OAIC	Office of the Australian Information Commissioner

Personal Information Security & Systems Architecture

PHI	Protected Health Information
PaaS	Platform as a Service
PbD	Privacy by Design
PIA	Privacy Impact Assessment
PII	Personally Identifiable Information
PIMS	Personal Information Management System
PIPEDA	Personal Information Protection and Electronic Documents Act
SaaS	Software as a Service
SAR	Subject Access Request
SDL, SDLC	Secure Development Lifecycle
SDLC	Software Development Lifecycle
S-SDLC	Secure Software Development Lifecycle
SDN	Software Defined Network
SEM	Security Event Management
SIEM	Security Information and Event Management
SOAR	Security Orchestration, Automation and Response
SOC	Service Organizational Control, System On Chip
UEBA	User & Entity Behaviour Analysis

Index

ABOUT THE AUTHOR

Keith Marlow has been involved in the Internet since 1996 and currently runs his own consultancy focussing on Systems Architecture and Security at scale.

Keith has twenty plus years' experience designing, developing, implementing, operating and securing large web sites and all the infrastructure that goes with them.

Prior to setting up Aykira, Keith was the Chief Architect of Asia for Yahoo! APAC. Where he was also the team lead for the application security engineers. He also ran the regional Architect training course and was a regional internationalisation expert.

Keith is a full member of both the Australian and British computer societies and holds both a PhD in Information Systems and a BSc Honours Degree in Computer Science.

linkedin.com/in/keithmarlow/
aykira.com.au

www.ingramcontent.com/pod-product-compliance
Lightning Source LLC
Chambersburg PA
CBHW071106050326
40690CB00008B/1132